DISCARDED FROM THE
NASHVILLE PUBLIC LIBRARY

D0752669

**Neil Gregor** is Reader in Modern German History at the University of Southampton. He is the author of *Daimler-Benz in the Third Reich* and editor of *Nazism: A Reader* and *Nazism, War and Genocide*. He is also currently writing a book on Nuremberg and the Nazi Past after 1945.

# HOW TO READ

# HITLER

NEIL GREGOR

**W. W. Norton & Company**
New York   London

First published in Great Britain by Granta Publications

Copyright © 2005 by Neil Gregor
First American Edition 2005

All rights reserved
Printed in the United States of America

*Mein Kampf* by Adolf Hitler, translated by Ralph Manheim. Copyright
© 1943, renewed 1971 by Houghton Mifflin Company. Reprinted by
permission of Houghton Mifflin Company. All rights reserved. Extracts
from *Mein Kampf*, translated by Ralph Manheim, published by Pimlico.
Used by permission of The Random House Group Limited. Extracts
from the *Second Book* reprinted with permission of the State of Bavaria.

For information about permission to reproduce selections from
this book, write to Permissions, W. W. Norton & Company, Inc.,
500 Fifth Avenue, New York, N.Y. 10110

Manufacturing by The Maple-Vail Book Manufacturing Group
Production manager: Amanda Morrison

Library of Congress Cataloging-in-Publication Data

Gregor, Neil, 1969–
How to read Hitler / Neil Gregor.— 1st American ed.
p. cm.—(How to read)
Includes bibliographical references and index.
**ISBN 0-393-32818-X (pbk.)**
1. Hitler, Adolf, 1889–1945—Political and social views. 2. Hitler, Adolf,
1889–1945—Psychology. 3. Hitler, Adolf, 1889–1945—Language.
4. Ideology—Germany—History—20th century. I. Title.
II. How to read (New York, N.Y.)
DD247.H5G678 2005
943.086'092—dc22
2005019137

W. W. Norton & Company, Inc.
500 Fifth Avenue, New York, N.Y. 10110
www.wwnorton.com

W. W. Norton & Company Ltd.
Castle House, 75/76 Wells Street, London W1T 3QT

1 2 3 4 5 6 7 8 9 0

# CONTENTS

# SERIES EDITOR'S FOREWORD

## How am I to read *How to Read*?

This series is based on a very simple, but novel idea. Most beginners' guides to great thinkers and writers offer either potted biography or condensed summaries of their major works, or perhaps even both. *How to Read*, by contrast, brings the reader face-to-face with the writing itself in the company of an expert guide. Its starting point is that in order to get close to what a writer is all about, you have to get close to the words they actually use and be shown how to read those words.

Every book in the series is in a way a masterclass in reading. Each author has selected ten or so short extracts from a writer's work and looks at them in detail as a way of revealing their central ideas and thereby opening doors onto a whole world of thought. Sometimes these extracts are arranged chronologically to give a sense of a thinker's development over time, sometimes not. The books are not merely compilations of a thinker's most famous passages, their 'greatest hits', but rather they offer a series of clues or keys that will enable readers to go on and make discoveries of their own. In addition to the texts and readings, each book provides a short biographical chronology and suggestions for further reading, internet resources, and so on. The books in the *How to Read* series don't claim to tell you all you need to know about Freud, Nietzsche and Darwin, or indeed Shakespeare and the Marquis de Sade, but they do offer the best starting point for further exploration.

Unlike the available second-hand versions of the minds that have shaped our intellectual, cultural, religious, political and scientific landscape, *How to Read* offers a refreshing set of first-hand encounters with those minds. Our hope is that these books will, by turn, instruct, intrigue, embolden, encourage and delight.

Simon Critchley
New School for Social Research, New York

# WHY READ HITLER?

Why should we read Hitler? Certainly not for his qualities as a writer. His prose is notorious for its grammatical inadequacies, its obscure South German idioms and its ill-phrased, ambiguous sentences. It gains nothing in translation, as generations of English-speaking historians have complained. 'Turgid', 'monotonous', and 'repetitive' are the familiar terms that successive commentators have used to convey something of the flavour of his prose.★

★ A note on the translations used in this book: excerpts from *Mein Kampf* are taken from *Hitler's Mein Kampf*, tr. Ralph Manheim, intr. by D.C. Watt (Hutchinson, 1974). Excerpts from Hitler's *Second Book* are taken, unless otherwise indicated, from Gerhard L. Weinberg (ed.), *Hitler's Second Book*, tr. Krista Smith (Enigma Books, 2003). This new version, although arguably guilty – despite its own claims – of polishing Hitler's prose in places, represents a considerably more accurate rendering than the unreliable 1961 translation (*Hitler's Secret Book*, tr. Salvator Attanasio, intr. by Telford Taylor [Grove Press, 1961]). I have, however, modified the 2003 translation in places, especially where this seemed necessary to capture adequately the violence of Hitler's prose. As Victor Klemperer described so vividly in *The Language of the Third Reich* (Athlone Press, 2000) violence was deeply embedded in all aspects of Nazi discourse, and any attempt to translate or to read Hitler's writings must take note of this essential characteristic.

Neither can one claim that Hitler was an original thinker. There is little in his writing or speeches that we cannot find in the penny pamphlets of pre-1914 Vienna where he began to form his political views. His racial anti-Semitism rehearses the familiar slogans of many on the pre-war right. His visions of German expansion echo the ideas of the more extreme wing of the radical-nationalist Pan German movement, which aimed at a German-dominated Central Europe from the late nineteenth century onwards, although it is true that his intended means were more aggressive than most. And, in essence, his anti-democratic, anti-Socialist sentiments similarly reproduce the conventional thinking of broad sectors of the German right from both before and after the First World War.

Some, indeed, would deny Hitler the status of 'thinker' at all. Alan Bullock, one of Hitler's first post-war biographers, refers to his 'moral and intellectual cretinism', while Joachim Fest dismisses his ideology as a combination of the anti-Semitism of the gutter and 'the sum of the clichés current in Vienna at the turn of the century'. His work certainly has none of the philosophical or intellectual rigour of the writings of contemporaries of the opposite ideological hue – of Lenin, Trotsky, or Bukharin. The reader will not struggle to find logical inconsistencies and self-contradiction. Some passages border on the incomprehensible.

On the other hand, academic commentators have often been too swift to dismiss the possibility that Hitler's writings might express an internally coherent view of the world. Justified moral condemnation has often been conflated – perhaps understandably – with intellectual condescension. Professional historians, trained to think rigorously and methodically, often forget that first-class thinkers are not the only thinkers, and certainly not always the most influential; they wrongly assume that just because someone cannot write it means that they have nothing to say, and forget that the inability to express oneself on paper does not mean that one does not believe what one thinks. As subsequent events were to show, this was far from being the case with Hitler.

Should we, though, read Hitler at all? His writing is neither uplifting nor inspirational − except perhaps for incorrigible extremists on the far right of contemporary politics. It preaches a message of hatred, violence and destruction. It offers a vision that, at a particular historical moment, became the focus for a massive popular mobilization of national, ethnic, social and cultural resentments − in the form of the National Socialist movement − that, sweeping away the fragile constitutional, political and legal safeguards of human rights in Germany, paved the way for a uniquely destructive war and a genocide that has become the yardstick for crimes against humanity in the modern era. Hitler's writing offers, in short, no starting points for the pursuit of peaceful, democratic, humane politics.

Yet this is, arguably, precisely the point. If we wish to understand how the National Socialist genocide of the Jews occurred − the political and ethical necessity of which study remains acute − it is with National Socialist ideology that we must start. For sure, an analysis of National Socialist doctrine offers only part of an answer to this broader problem, which also demands historical consideration of the material and cultural legacies of the First World War, the processes of fascist mobilization from the 1920s through to the 1930s, the erosion of the rule of law under the impact of the charismatic 'Führer State', the creation of a genocidal moral climate and so on. But, equally, an analysis of the events of the Second World

War and the Holocaust which did not place some emphasis on the core ideological principles and ambitions of the National Socialist movement would be partial and inadequate at best. National Socialist ideology might not have had the theoretical sophistication or subtlety of the various strands of Marxist thought that emerged over the nineteenth and twentieth centuries, but its leading figures subscribed to a system of thought of sorts; moreover, the values which that system of thought contained were those that informed the ethos of the broader National Socialist movement.

Furthermore, recent developments in the interpretation of Nazism have made it a timely moment for those interested in explaining the horrors of the Third Reich to return to *Mein Kampf*. For example, the move away from a one-sided stress on institutional conflict as the principal motor of National Socialist radicalization in favour of a renewed emphasis on the importance of human agency, and on cooperation and 'shared understanding' between actors, suggests a need to return to the basic tenets of National Socialist belief. Similarly, the gradual shift away from older theories of a German 'Special Path' stretching back to Bismarck, with their emphasis on political, institutional and social continuities going back at least to the first modern unification of Germany in 1871, in favour of an interpretation which places more weight on the profound political, social and cultural shocks brought about by the First World War should encourage us to ask: in what ways might *Mein Kampf* be seen as a document of that shock?

For the historian, approaching the words of Hitler is, unfortunately, anything but straightforward. To start with, as is well known, Hitler was extremely averse to writing anything down. As a result, many key sources for understanding his thinking at any given moment take the form of memoranda or diary entries composed by others, rather than words written by Hitler himself. The Hossbach memorandum of 5 November 1937, in which are recorded Hitler's thoughts on the possible future evolution of German foreign policy, is one famous example of this; similarly, much of our knowledge of Hitler's thinking during the Second World War comes from sources such as General Halder's diaries rather than from anything that Hitler wrote. Even Hitler's most famous pieces of prose were dictated rather than written by him – which perhaps partly accounts for the awfulness of some of their phrasing. *Mein Kampf*, which was produced during Hitler's incarceration in the Landsberg prison following his first abortive attempt at seizing power in the Munich putsch of 1923, and published in two parts in 1925 and 1926, was created in this way. The same is true of Hitler's much less well known but nonetheless very important *Second Book*. Moreover, his *Second Book*, which was written in 1928 and which in many ways offers the clearest and most succinct statement of his views on many issues, remained unpublished during Hitler's lifetime. This raises further questions about how much importance we should accord it, especially as it bears all the hallmarks of an unfinished manuscript.

More fundamentally, the intensely oral nature of the political culture of the Third Reich was such that most people's contact with Hitler's thinking was through his speeches rather than through his writings. The centrality of the spoken as distinct from the written word to the creation of Hitler's charisma was such that, if we are to understand fully the place, function and significance of ideology within the Nazi political system and in its political aesthetic, and indeed the circulation of ideology in German society in general at that time, we need to give due weight to a consideration of Hitler's speeches as well as his writings. But should we read them as being of equal importance to Hitler's writings? Should we read them in the same way? Should we accord them the same status when seeking to understand Hitler's 'world-view'? Given the absence of a substantial body of formal written work from Hitler's own hand, the historian obviously relies upon such texts when thinking about all sorts of individual problems of interpretation, but he or she has to remember that they were conceived and delivered as pieces of oratory, not as political tracts, and thus originally performed in very different ways to their original audiences than if they had been created to be read. For all the obvious rhetorical properties of a text such as *Mein Kampf*, which also bears many hallmarks of its time of writing, such distinctions of genre always have to be borne in mind. Speeches were usually written for the moment, and served specific purposes for their audiences both inside and outside the arena in which they were delivered. Few would accept that Hitler's protestations of his peaceful intentions in the early and mid-1930s should be seen as serious statements of his political ambitions or ideological beliefs, for example.

While a consideration of the spoken as well as the written word is thus crucial in understanding fully the processes by which ideas circulated through the Third Reich, and while Hitler's speeches were undoubtedly far more important to the creation of his charisma in the 1930s and 1940s than anything he wrote that appeared in print, the search for the ideological origins of the war and genocide for which National Socialism was responsible is best pursued through a consideration of his writings. As a result, this book concentrates on those writings rather than on Hitler's speeches.

How, then, should we read Hitler? The challenges are exemplified by the following sentence from Hitler's *Second Book*. It offers an example of Hitler's prose which, although not chosen at random, is quite representative of his writing:

> If a really vigorous people believes that it cannot conquer another with peaceful economic means, or if an economically weaker people does not wish to let itself be killed by an economically stronger one, as its ability to feed itself is slowly cut off, then in both cases the mist of peaceful economic phraseology will be suddenly torn apart and war, that is the continuation of politics by other means, steps into its place.*
>
> (2B, 22–3)

Reading this hopelessly unstructured string of clauses one can picture Hitler standing, peering over the shoulders of his hapless scribe, forming sentences as ideas come into his head and inserting sub-clauses as the thoughts and associations randomly strike him. There is an unmistakably 'stream of consciousness' quality to the writing, which does not appear to have undergone even the most basic editing, let alone anything like rigorous polishing. It also contains an almost impossibly clumsy mixed metaphor – what is 'the mist of peaceful economic phraseology'? And how does one tear mist apart?

---

* I have chosen to use a modified version of the less-well-regarded 1961 translation here as it seems to me to capture better the poverty of the original prose, which has been improved in the 2003 translation to the point where the mixed metaphor has been entirely removed. The page reference refers to the 1961 edition.

The sentence does, however, contain several assumptions about history and politics that reflect Hitler's views in general. First, there is the division of the world into strong and weak peoples, and the sense that the former are naturally inclined to try to conquer the latter. Second, Hitler implies that economics is only superficially the motive for conflict, that it only works to a limited extent as an explanation – and, indeed, can obfuscate the real picture. Ultimately, conflicts are decided by war. The reader might also detect a key reference: 'war is the continuation of politics by other means' comes from the Prussian military thinker Clausewitz. It serves to remind us, then, that Hitler did draw on the thoughts and writings of others in forming his views. And, finally, the language itself resonates with violence, not only in the obvious reference to peoples settling their conflicts by war and killing, but in the image of things being 'suddenly torn apart'. This is not an accidental image, but says much about the mentality of its author, who was, first and foremost, a man of violence.

Analysing Hitler's prose passage by passage, line by line is not, in any case, always the best way to extract from the texts the meanings that are undoubtedly there. Much of the interpretative challenge lies in appreciating the significance of the simple but extensive sets of synonyms and antonyms that Hitler uses throughout his writing. When Hitler refers to democracy, he associates this with the Jews. When Hitler mentions the malign influence of the press, he is also thinking of Jews. When Hitler says 'Marxist', he yet again means 'Jew'. This is demonstrated most tellingly by the constant use of compound or hyphenated expressions such as 'Jewish-democratic', 'Jewish-Bolshevik', or 'pacifist-Marxist' and 'democratic-pacifist'. 'Socialist', 'Democrat',

'Pacifist', 'Internationalist' – these are to be understood as interchangeable terms. Ominously, so are their associations with a related set of near-synonyms – 'criminal', 'betrayer', 'traitor' and so on. These, in turn, are associated with a clear set of vices: corruption, materialism, selfishness, mendaciousness, cowardice. 'The German', by contrast, is associated with all the opposing virtues – honesty, idealism, selflessness, bravery, self-sacrifice.

Second, central to all Hitler's writings is a set of simple but overarching metaphors through which his entire political analysis is expressed. The military metaphors encapsulate Hitler's conception of politics; the biological metaphors contain both his understanding of the causes of national strength and national weakness, and the implicitly genocidal message contained within the vision as a whole. These are rarely spelled out, but are constantly present in references to the 'national body' or to 'illnesses' and the need for 'antidotes'. Indeed, perhaps the greatest interpretative challenge for the reader lies in distinguishing what, for Hitler, was real, and what was metaphorical: distinctions which are clear in the mind of the historian or literary critic may have been less clear in the mind of Hitler himself. Either way, the paucity of thought and tortuousness of the prose on a line-by-line basis notwithstanding, there is a crude system of ideas present in Hitler's writings that the careful student will be able to analyse. As the historian R.C.K. Ensor said of *Mein Kampf* at a lecture delivered at the Royal Institute of International Affairs in 1939, 'any subject may turn up on almost any page', but 'while it lacks logical sequence, it by no means lacks logic.'

Reading Hitler, then, is not like reading Shakespeare. But it is still a fruitful experience for those wishing to begin to understand how the National Socialist genocide of Europe's

Jews originated. This book introduces the reader to the ways in which historians might go about reading the writings of one of the most influential figures of the twentieth century. Focusing on extracts from *Mein Kampf* and the *Second Book* – some of which have been selected as key passages, others because they work well as examples that are typical of what are highly repetitive texts – it shows how the patient reader can detect in Hitler's writings both the presence of a genocidal mentality and the statement of an implicitly genocidal message.

In some cases the extracts have been chosen because they yield up much through detailed scrutiny. In others, they have been chosen because they offer good starting points for thinking about aspects of the texts as a whole. Some have been selected because they stimulate interesting reflections upon the relationship of Hitler's world-view to broader currents of nineteenth- and early twentieth-century thought. Some have been selected because the contrast between the traditionalist nationalist rhetoric being deployed and the modernity of the fascist vision being espoused – this contrast is a key feature of *Mein Kampf* – is particularly striking. Some are used because they suggest something broader about the impact of the First World War on German political culture; others because they typify what is unique to Hitler. The emphasis will be on suggesting that Hitler's writing, alternating between the sickening and the soporific as it undoubtedly does, can still be read in many different ways for many different purposes.

# 2

# THE POLITICS OF GENRE

The most notorious political tract ever written opens with the following passage:

> Today it seems to me providential that Fate should have chosen Braunau on the Inn as my birthplace. For this little town lies on the boundary between two German states which we of the younger generation at least have made it our life work to reunite by every means at our disposal.
>
> German-Austria must return to the great German mother country, and not because of any economic considerations. No, and again no: even if such a union were unimportant from an economic point of view; yes, even if it were harmful, it must nevertheless take place. One blood demands one Reich. Never will the German nation possess the moral right to engage in colonial politics until, at least, it embraces its own sons within a single state. Only when the Reich borders include the very last German, but can no longer guarantee his daily bread, will the moral right to acquire foreign soil arise from the distress of our own people. Their sword will become our plough, and from the

tears of war the daily bread of future generations will grow.
And so this little city on the border seems to me the symbol
of a great mission

(MK, 3)

The reflections on the historical accident of Hitler's border-
lands birthplace with which *Mein Kampf* opens offer, in many
ways, an example in miniature of the reading challenges posed
by the text as a whole. They are awkwardly punctuated, bear-
ing all the hallmarks of someone whose thoughts are still
forming as he is speaking; their tone is extremely pompous;
their crude personifying imagery of the German nation (the
'mother' nation who 'embraces' her sons) introduces the
reader to a tortuous literary style which only the most com-
mitted will be willing to endure for a further six hundred
pages. Moreover, the uncompromising tone ('no and again
no', 'by every means at our disposal', 'one blood demands one
Reich') forewarns the reader that this is anything but a careful, considered discussion of German politics. It is as much
bombastic rant as structured critique, more a string of wilful
assertions than a set of cogent arguments.

Small wonder, then, that so many commentators have been
so dismissive. However, for those able to tolerate the punishing
prose style, these lines yield up much of interest. Indeed many,
if not all, of the themes and issues which resonate through Hitler's
writings can be discerned in these first two hundred words.

Most obviously, these opening lines of *Mein Kampf* contain
many of the central tenets of Hitler's ideological world-view.
Firstly, there is the fixation on issues of race. Foreign policy
must be driven by racial necessities, not by economics; membership of the nation, or race, is conferred by ties of blood;
the boundaries of the state should embrace all members of the

race. The state, so runs the clear implication, is there not to serve the dynastic interests of the ruling family but the needs of the nation as a whole. What is being introduced, in other words, is a populist rather than a patrician view of politics. The task of the state is to feed the members of the race, and when that is no longer possible the state has the right to pursue a policy of expansion. That expansion, however, should not be undertaken through the pursuit of overseas colonies but through acquisition of territory adjacent to the mother country. Such expansion can and should be pursued by military means, and will secure the basis for future prosperity.

Even these few lines suffice, then, to reveal to the reader that they have embarked upon a text of political philosophy whose preoccupations with issues of race, nation, military expansion and empire place it within a nineteenth- and early twentieth-century tradition that draws on the thought of several earlier writers. The fixation with race places Hitler within an unappealing intellectual and philosophical lineage that one can trace back to Gobineau, whose *Essay on the Inequality of Human Races* (1854) stands as the founding text of modern racist ideology. The interest in war as a central tool of state politics continues a tradition which, as we have already observed, one can trace immediately back to the Prussian military thinker Clausewitz, whose treatise *On War* (1832) was very familiar to Hitler. In his affirmation of the allegedly creative, positive impact of imperial conquest we can also see the direct influence of Houston Stewart Chamberlain, whose abysmal *Foundations of the Nineteenth Century* (1898) was another key text in the formation of Hitler's world-view.

We shall return to consider Hitler's reading and thinking habits at greater length in a later chapter. We should note from the outset, however, that from *Mein Kampf*'s first page onwards his writings are revealed not as the work of a marginal figure who entered German history from outside pre-existing political, philosophical or intellectual traditions but as the creations of someone whose preoccupations place him firmly within an established canon of racist, nationalist and militarist thought stretching back over a century. To dismiss Hitler's ideas as merely eccentric or deranged is intellectually and morally lazy – it enables us to talk about Hitler in a way that avoids raising more awkward questions about the genealogy of his beliefs or their place within the intellectual traditions of western modernity.

Yet there is much more to this opening passage than an introductory statement of Hitler's political philosophy. Whilst ruminating on matters of race and empire, after all, it simultaneously introduces the reader to another key facet of his writing: his preoccupation with history. Much of Hitler's work takes the form of extended reflections on both world history in general and German history in particular. The scholar seeking to discern Hitler's own political ambitions in his texts will often find that they are implicit in his discussion of history rather than explicitly stated in their own right – Hitler spent as much time describing what was wrong with past policy decisions as he did outlining his own prescriptions, and how much we think we can learn about Hitler's intentions depends on how much we are willing to take as implicit in these criticisms.

How, then, should we read this passage as a reflection on history? On the one hand, clearly, it embodies the belief in a golden mythical past. In announcing the ambition to 'reunite' the 'two German states' of Germany and Austria, and in its use of the language of 'return', it harks back to an imagined historical moment of national or ethnic unity which, so we divine, Hitler intends to restore. Quite when Hitler regards this mythical moment of unity as having existed is unclear, but one imagines that he is referring to the medieval first German Reich. It is more important, though, to note the general point: Hitler constantly drew on images of a positive past – be they of the medieval Reich, of the wars of Frederick the Great in the eighteenth century, or the anti-French enthusiasms of the early nineteenth-century 'Wars of Liberation' – to contrast the strength and potential of the German nation with its recent decline and its current sorry state.

This, in turn, underlines the other aspect of Hitler's historical approach – his practice of describing political and ideological aspirations in terms of a critical narrative of the more recent past. Most obviously, the demand that Germany and Austria be reunited represents a rejection of the peace terms imposed by the victorious powers of the First World War in the Treaty of Versailles of 1919. The treaty's stipulation that there should be no *Anschluss*, or union, between the two states inflamed nationalist opinion throughout Germany in the immediate post-First World War era. But in demanding the union of all Germans on the basis of ethnic identity Hitler is also implicitly criticizing the manner in which Germany was unified in 1871. Competing visions of the best way to unify the fragmented German nation into a single state had circulated amongst nationalists throughout the nineteenth century: some had preferred a 'little German' solution – excluding Catholic Austria – under the domination of Protestant Prussia, while others had pushed for a 'greater Germany' under Austrian leadership. For advocates of a 'greater German' union such as Hitler, the Prussian-led 'little German' solution engineered by Bismarck was only a half measure, because it did not include all Germans. This is not to say that Hitler was a fierce critic of Bismarck, who is generally praised in Hitler's writings as a shrewd diplomat with a strong sense of the politically possible. But Hitler did regard the 'little German' solution as inadequate, as merely a stage in a greater process of national consciousness-building and national expansion.

Hitler was, moreover, very critical of Bismarck's successors, whom he regarded as having squandered the 'Iron Chancellor's' legacy. Long passages of Hitler's writings take the form of an extended critique of the political decisions of the late-nineteenth century: of what he saw as Germany's mistaken alliance policy or as the wrongful pursuit of overseas colonies. In rejecting engagement in colonial politics in this opening passage Hitler is directly criticizing the late-nineteenth-century statesmen for their pursuit of *Weltpolitik*, or 'world policy', over Continental expansion, thus raising a theme to which he returns time and time again in both *Mein Kampf* and the *Second Book*: the need to avoid a policy of trade-based colonialism which would (and, Hitler believed, did) inevitably lead Germany into military confrontation with Britain.

Yet this passage does not confine its comments on economics to a rejection of the trade-based colonialism embodied in the pursuit of *Weltpolitik*. It rejects more generally the notion that state policy should be driven by economic concerns, and explicitly asserts that the state should be willing to take decisions even when they run counter to economic rationality or the needs of the economy. This, in turn, alerts us to another aspect of Hitler's approach to history – his tendency to couch discussions of politics in a critique of the negative impact of the industrial revolution and the advent of commerce-driven modernity. Whether

Hitler rejected industrial society in its entirety, or was merely critical of some of its negative effects and the failure of politicians to deal with them, is, again, a subject for debate and will be addressed in Chapter 8. There is no doubt, however, that Hitler rejected a world in which he saw both politics and the daily life of individuals as being excessively driven by commercial or materialistic prerogatives – time and time again he derided the 'mammonization' of contemporary life. And while it is not explicitly stated here, the reader will soon discover whom he blames: the Jews.

In its reflections on the past this passage thus introduces us to the doubled-sided nature of Hitler's view of history. On the one hand, he looked back to an ill-defined mythical golden past as a source of inspiration. On the other, he saw in the more recent German past a process of decline set in train by the advent of industrial modernity and the emergence of a commerce-driven world. This culture, he believed, was to blame for the wrong decisions of the bourgeois statesmen of the late nineteenth century. The emergence of the liberal values of commerce and trade-based prosperity which Hitler rejected had been to blame both for a mistaken foreign policy that had led to war with Britain and for a political culture that did not adequately prepare Germans to fight. The result was defeat, division, the loss of territory and imposed separation, against which Hitler set the vision of a reunified Germany and a heroic future.

It is in this vision of recent history as decline and the future as renewal that we can see what is specifically fascist about this passage. Hitler reveals himself not only as a nationalist politician and a racist thinker, but – this is a central characteristic of fascist ideology – as offering a vision of revitalization and *rebirth* following the perceived decay of the liberal era, whose failings he intends to overcome. The text functions as a means of positioning himself in relation not just to the Treaty of Versailles, and by extension to the fledgling democratic German government that signed it, but in relation to the bourgeois age as a whole. Hitler is announcing his presence as a new species of politician driven not by the priorities of nineteenth-century commercialism but by the needs of the race, and specifically by its need for regeneration. In other words, for all his assertion of a mythical distant past, this opening passage is not advocating a return to the status quo ante of 1914, and should not be regarded as articulating a reactionary, restorative vision for Germany – Hitler is making it clear that his politics are of a new kind.

But if discussion of the narratives of the past embedded in the text of *Mein Kampf* alerts us to the way in which it functions simultaneously as political philosophy and as history, then it should be emphasized that these are not the only two literary genres that the book embodies. Both the title of the work and the first sentence of this opening passage introduce us to the third and in some ways most important genre: the book announces itself, and is structured as, an autobiography. The opening chapter is entitled 'In the House of My Parents'; subsequent chapter headings introduce Hitler's 'Years of Study and Suffering in Vienna', his time in 'Munich', his experiences of 'The World War' and 'The Beginning of My Political Activity' before going on to outline the early history of the National Socialist party. Hitler's views on history and politics are woven into the autobiographical structure (in digressions that are admittedly often very lengthy). The dominant motif, as the title of the book suggests, is 'struggle'.

As autobiography – as it is conventionally understood – or as an account of the early years of the National Socialist party and Hitler's role within it *Mein Kampf* is notoriously unreliable. Simple dates, such as that of his move from Vienna to Munich, are wrongly given – Hitler claimed that he went to Munich in 1912, whereas in truth he went in 1913. Stories are invented, such as that of an alleged encounter with Viennese Social Democratic workers when he was working as a labourer on a building site. Others, such as his account of his first conscious encounter with a Jew, are so stylized as to be manifestly untrue. Hitler misrepresents his role in the very early phase of the National Socialist party's history, claiming to have been given membership number 7 when in fact he became member number 555, and he is constantly inaccurate in his dating of early party meetings or of the numbers in attendance at such events.

Some of these errors may reflect Hitler's lack of attention to detail, some of them are unimportant and some may indeed be honest mistakes. But, in any case, it is not as autobiography in the strict sense of the word that we should be reading *Mein Kampf*. We can only understand the 'autobiographical' nature of the text if we stop to consider the political circumstances under which it was written, and the state of Hitler's political career at that time.

The far-right nationalist political milieu from which Hitler and the National Socialist movement emerged in the early 1920s was fragmented and faction-ridden. As well as the Bavarian-based National Socialist party there existed, for example, the *Deutschvölkische Schutz- und Trutzbund* (The German Racist Protection and Defiance League), the *Deutschsozialistische Partei* (The German Socialist Party), and the *Deutschvölkische Freiheitspartei* (The German Racist Freedom Party). In addition, there were the many right-wing paramilitary units such as the Ehrhardt Brigade. Many later prominent figures in the National Socialist regime began their political careers in these rival groups. Julius Streicher, for example, who was later to gain notoriety as the viciously anti-Semitic *Gauleiter* of Franconia, transferred his allegiance from the *DSP* in 1922. Sometimes these rival groups came together under brief-lived umbrella organizations such as the *Deutsche Kampfbund* (The German Combat League), which formed the basis for Hitler's Munich putsch of 1923; but usually such displays of unity could not survive the conflicts that constantly flared up between their constituent elements.

Following the Munich putsch, the German far right had fragmented once more. The *Deutschvölkische Freiheitspartei* continued its separate existence while the National Socialist party fell into some disarray. Many within the National Socialist party were in favour of merging with the DVFP into a *Nationalsozialistische Freiheitspartei* (National Socialist Freedom Party). Even following his release from Landsberg prison in December 1924, Hitler struggled for some time to gain control over north German members of the National Socialist party who had their own agendas and their own ambitions for power. The point is that at the time of writing *Mein Kampf* Hitler was far from being the undisputed leader of the far right that he was later to become.

Armed with this knowledge, we can see that the autobiographical account – with its emphasis on 'destiny', 'fate' and (in this opening passage) 'providence' – serves a clear political purpose. Far from offering a dispassionate account of Hitler's early years, it is intended to project an image of Hitler as the most dynamic, uncompromising, radical figure on the far right, and thus to underpin his bid for leadership of the extremist scene. This was, indeed, the period in which the myth of Hitler as the predestined *Führer* began to emerge.

Read in this light, the reworking of an historical accident –
Hitler's birth in Braunau on the Inn – into the 'symbol of a
great mission' is not merely a superficial rhetorical flourish, it
is the beginning of a carefully crafted representation of the
author's own life in which everything is seen as leading up to
his takeover of first the leadership of the German right and
then, by implication, the whole German nation.

Hitler pursues this strategy throughout the entire book.
His account in the pages that follow of his conflicts with his
father – 'barely eleven years old, I was forced into opposition
for the first time in my life' (MK, 7) – while not totally devoid
of truth becomes just one of a number of elements in Hitler's
life that are rewritten to fit in with the image of a figure chosen
by fate to emerge as the hardest and strongest opponent of
the hated Weimar Republic. We also learn, for example, that:
'I believe that even then my oratorical talent was being
developed in the form of more or less violent arguments with
my schoolmates' (MK, 5), or that: 'I wanted to become an archi-
tect, and obstacles do not exist to be surrendered to, but only
to be broken' (MK, 19). The uncompromising tone that Hitler
adopts is thus not merely the general expression of a defiant
personality but a statement of his refusal to see the dynamism
of his party diluted by cooperation with 'bourgeois' right-wing
elements which he sees as insufficiently radical. The description
of himself and his followers as 'we of the younger generation' is
also a conscious attempt to distinguish his disciples from other
right-wing groups. Mergers are rejected: only through
unequivocal submission to the leadership of Hitler himself will
the right be able to fulfil its ambitions for the whole nation.

For all its awkwardness of style, therefore, *Mein Kampf*
reveals itself immediately to be a very rich source of material
for the historian. As a tract of political philosophy, it

announces itself from the outset as belonging to certain traditions of right-wing nationalist, militarist and racist thought. As a representation of history it reveals Hitler as a fascist ideologue seeking German national rebirth following a period of decay that is associated with the politics of the bourgeois era. As an autobiography it reveals Hitler's own emerging sense of his political destiny and his attempts to stamp his authority over the faction-ridden world of the far right in the immediate aftermath of the First World War. The generic forms that the text takes are, in short, no accident, but are laden with political meanings.

## 3

## LANGUAGE AND POLITICS

Having first asserted his dominance over the German far right, and then gained power over Germany as a whole, what did Hitler intend to do next? When, if at all, did his ambition to embark upon expansionism and mass murder crystallize, and how?

In addressing the question of when Hitler formed his 'world-view', historians have tended to debate whether his views were largely formed in the environment of pre-First World War Vienna – as he himself claims in *Mein Kampf* – or whether they were still evolving in the early and mid-1920s. *Mein Kampf* has also been read, of course, for the clues that it offers to the events of the 1930s and 1940s. But whether we see in it a blueprint for the invasion of the Soviet Union and the mass murder of Europe's Jews or merely the announce-ment of a more general set of anti-Semitic and expansionist ambitions, we should remember to read the text not only for what it might tell us about what Hitler intended to do when he came to power but also for what it might tell us about the time in which it was written. Perhaps most importantly in this context, we need to read *Mein Kampf* for what it might tell us about the impact of the First World War both on Hitler's thinking and on German society. Indeed, arguably the key starting point for understanding Hitler's most important text lies precisely in a close reading of what he has to say about that war, in which he fought as an ordinary, anonymous soldier for four years.

Consider the following passage:

> At last the day came when we left Munich to begin the fulfilment of our duty. For the first time I saw the Rhine as we rode westward along its quiet waters to defend it, the German stream of streams, from the greed of the old enemy. When through the tender veil of the early morning mist the Niederwald Monument gleamed down upon us in the gentle first rays of the sun, the old 'Watch on the Rhine' roared out of the endless transport train into the morning sky, and I felt as though my heart would burst.
>
> And then came a damp, cold night in Flanders, through which we marched in silence, and when the day began to emerge from the mists, suddenly an iron greeting came whizzing at us over our heads, and with a sharp report sent the little pellets flying between our ranks, ripping up the wet ground; but even before the little cloud had passed, from two hundred throats the first hurrah rose to meet the first messenger of death. Then a crackling and a roaring, a singing and a howling began, and with feverish eyes each one of us was drawn forward, faster and faster, until suddenly past turnip fields and hedges the fight began, the fight of man against man. And from the distance the strains of a song reached our ears, coming closer and closer, leaping from company to company, and just as Death plunged a busy hand into our

ranks, the song reached us too and we passed it along:
'*Deutschland, Deutschland über Alles, über Alles in der Welt!*'

(MK, 150–1)

These crudely lyrical evocations of the mobilization of Germany's troops in 1914 offer a typical example of the pervasive nationalist mythologies engendered by the First World War. For Hitler, as for many of his generation who fought as ordinary soldiers, the war was an inspirational experience. First, there was the wave of patriotism which led idealistic young Germans to rush to the colours to defend the fatherland. As this passage strikingly shows, this patriotic fervour and its subsequent mythologization drew strongly on the traditional anti-French rhetoric of nineteenth-century German nationalism. The 'Watch on the Rhine' is a song written by Max Schneckenburger in 1840 to celebrate patriotic opposition to the French during the 'War Scare on the Rhine', when ordinary Germans stood guard on the Rhine in response to fears of French invasion in that year; the Niederwald Monument, near Koblenz, which Hitler alleges he passed on the way to Flanders was one of Germany's most famous nationalist commemorations of victory in the Franco–Prussian War of 1870–71.

Second, the passage captures something of the nationalist myths of unity created by the war itself – the sense that German men of all classes marched together to defend the common home. As ever, it is not easy to separate those elements which represent Hitler's personal experience from his tendency to restate general myths of the war experience: the image of new recruits singing '*Deutschland, Deutschland über Alles*' as they march cheerfully towards the French guns has more than a faint echo of the famous events in the autumn of 1914 at Langemarck, where young student volunteers met their deaths in similar fashion and were subsequently immortalized in nationalist mythology. This reminds us, again, not to see in *Mein Kampf* a literal account of Hitler's personal experiences but a hybrid text whose autobiographical narrative is inextricably fused with its radical nationalist message.

For the far right this moment of unity, at which all class barriers and distinctions were transcended, was perpetuated in the 'socialism of the trenches', the community of soldiers in which each fought for the other and for Germany without regard for the origins or peacetime occupation of his comrade. This was a real 'socialism' forged in the blood of the trenches, not the false socialism foisted on unsuspecting workers by mendacious Jews. The spirit of community created in the trenches, moreover, was one which laughed in the face of death: it was the constant presence of death that fostered the masculine traits of 'hardness' and 'determination', captured in Hitler's image of the 'feverish eyes' of his comrades. The glorification of this trench experience, and the celebration of such masculine hardness was far from unique to Hitler. It was widespread in the popular literature of the post-war years: Ernst Jünger's novel *Storm of Steel* (1920) is one typical example. Finally, though, this passage is not merely an evocative assertion of masculine bravery in the face of violence – it glorifies the violence of war itself. The 'fight of man against man' was seen by fascists across Europe as having an ennobling quality in itself: the violence of war would, it was believed, have a cleansing effect on a national life which was increasingly decadent and rotten. Again, then, it is in such close reading that we may see in Hitler not merely another German nationalist but a representative of a new, specifically fascist mentality. For fascism was not only an ideology, but also a political style – a revolutionary new form of activism – to which violence and its glorification was absolutely central.

How significant, then, was the war in the formation of Hitler's mind? Tellingly, in describing one particularly violent beer-hall brawl with left-wing opponents in the early 1920s at which shots supposedly rang out, Hitler relates in *Mein Kampf* that 'your heart almost rejoiced at such a revival of old war experiences' (MK, 461). Beyond this, however, it is important to note just how profound the experience of war was on Hitler's political imagination. The entire text of *Mein Kampf* is infused with military language of one kind or another. Political life is described in terms of 'attack' and 'defence', with parties 'attacking and seizing the enemy position' (MK, 46) with arguments or methods always described as 'weapons'; political adversaries are not mere opponents but always 'enemies' or 'foes'. The urban poor are described as a 'menacing army' (MK, 38), while the working-class masses are the 'shock troops' of Marxism who in turn set out 'to storm an existing order' (MK, 343).

More specifically, it was the battlefields of the Western Front on which Hitler had fought that provided him with a set of images and vocabulary through which he imagined the entire terrain of post-war democratic politics. He describes his opponents on the left as unleashing a 'veritable barrage of lies and slanders . . . until the nerves of the attacked persons break down' (MK, 40); he speaks of the need, when dealing with political opponents, 'to combat poison gas with poison gas' (MK, 41); describing a beer-hall political riot of the early 1920s he tells us that beer mugs flew through the air 'like howitzer shells' (MK, 460). In one striking extended metaphor, Hitler scornfully describes the mass of would-be democratic politicians waiting for a coveted seat in parliament – and thus for access to all its corrupting material benefits – in terms of soldiers waiting to go over the top in the war: 'they stand in a long line, and with pain and regret count the number of those waiting ahead of them, calculating almost the precise hour at which, in all probability, their turn will come. Consequently, they long for any change in the office hovering before their eyes, and are thankful for any scandal which thins out the ranks ahead of them' (MK, 76). Such an image of democratic politicians as men anxious to go over the top sits uneasily with Hitler's constant associations of democracy and 'cowardice', or of democrats with pacifists desperate to remain on the home front, and suggests that Hitler has not quite thought through the implications of his comments, but it underlines how deeply embedded in his prose such militarized ways of seeing and thinking are.

It is undoubtedly in this context that we should read the following notorious sentence: 'If at the beginning of the War and during the War twelve or fifteen thousand of these Hebrew corrupters of the people had been held under poison gas, as happened to hundreds of thousands of our very best German workers in the field, the sacrifice of millions at the front would not have been in vain' (MK, 620). Hitler's use of the imagery is quite unsurprising, given that he himself was the victim of a gas attack towards the end of the war, and, while there is much in *Mein Kampf* which we might interpret as implicitly genocidal, this sentence does not form part of such evidence. To interpret it as such is to rely too much on hindsight. Instead, it is a further striking example of how the social and cultural impact of the First World War fostered the militarization of certain forms of German political rhetoric after 1918.

For Hitler's use of militaristic language should not be seen in isolation, but as indicative of a much wider crisis of political culture brought about by the cataclysmic conflagration of 1914–18. The impact of the First World War was not confined to influencing the language of the far right, but extended to far-reaching changes in political mobilization and activism in Germany more generally. The use of paramilitary squads to protect political meetings and engage in street violence with opponents, the use of uniforms, banners and parades, the singing of military or militaristic songs, the introduction of military patterns of authority and obedience into political parties, the use of military symbols and heroes in political imagery and rhetoric – all of these permeated the political culture of the 1920s and may be regarded as evidence of the widespread cultural legacies of the First World War. Hitler's writing, far from being unique, exceptional or even unusual, is instead quite typical in this respect.

The militaristic and violent imagery and rhetoric of *Mein Kampf* is, then, symptomatic of a broader cultural and political crisis engendered by the experience of the First World War. It gives us an insight not just into Hitler but into the violence of the politics of the 1920s more generally. However, we fail to do full justice to the significance of this language if we see it merely as symptomatic of something broader. The violent language of *Mein Kampf* does not just describe the past. Rather, as some of the First World War images themselves suggest, there also is more than an intimation of threatened *future* violence against those whom Hitler regards as Germany's enemies. The phrase 'a thirty-centimetre shell has always hissed more loudly than a thousand Jewish newspaper vipers – so let them hiss!' (MK, 224) is one telling example of such a passing comment in which Hitler (using anti-Semitic imagery whose precise meanings we shall again explore in chapter 6) not only deploys one of his many First World War images but threatens clearly to unleash that violence against the Jews.

Consider the following two short extracts:

> a) [My] position is that there is no use in hanging petty thieves in order to let big ones go free; but that some day a German national court must judge and execute some ten thousand of the organizing and hence responsible criminals of the November betrayal and everything that goes with it.
>
> (MK, 496)

> b) The soul of the people can only be won if along with carrying on a positive struggle for our own aims, we destroy the opponent of these aims.
>
> The people at all times see the proof of their own right in ruthless attack on a foe, and to them renouncing the destruction of the adversary seems like uncertainty with regard to their own right if not a sign of their own unright.
>
> The broad masses are only a piece of Nature and their sentiment does not understand the mutual handshake of people who claim that they want the opposite things. What they desire is the victory of the stronger and the destruction of the weak or his unconditional subjection.
>
> The nationalization of the masses will succeed only when, aside from all the positive struggle for the soul of our people, their international poisoners are exterminated.
>
> (MK, 307)

As we know, the National Socialist seizure of power was accompanied by a huge wave of political violence against the movement's opponents. So-called 'wild' concentration camps sprang up spontaneously overnight in working-class districts such as Berlin-Wedding. Within two months of Hitler's appointment as Chancellor in January 1933, the first official concentration camp had been set up in Dachau, just outside Munich. By the end of 1933, 150,000 Communists had been arrested, murdered or forced into exile. The concentration camp system expanded throughout the twelve years of National Socialism's rule into a sprawling network across the whole of Occupied Europe: it held many hundreds of thousands of prisoners in the later years of the Second World War.

Moreover, the persecution of the Jews also began immediately following Hitler's seizure of power. Boycotts, discriminatory legislation, social marginalization, random abuse and violence were inflicted upon Germany's Jews from 1933 onwards. Many were sent to concentration camps during the 1930s, and as German territorial expansion got under way serious persecution quickly spiralled into outright mass murder. From the beginning of the Second World War, Jews were murdered en masse in labour camps, ghettos and mass shootings; by the middle of the war, systematic genocide was under way in the extermination camps.

This knowledge raises the obvious question: is violence on this scale prefigured in *Mein Kampf*? Is mass murder of the type that subsequently took place implicit in the unremittingly aggressive tone? It would be idle to suggest that the two passages cited above, or indeed any others, can be read as a statement of the intention to establish concentration camps in

Dachau, Sachsenhausen, or anywhere else. Still less can we discern any plans to establish extermination camps at Auschwitz, Treblinka, or Belzec. Again, the case for seeing *Mein Kampf* as an implicitly genocidal text is a strong one, but it cannot be made in this simplistic way – such a reading rests too much on hindsight.

Nonetheless, there *is* an extreme language of violence contained in these and other passages, which is clearly not accidental. In the passage referring to the 'November criminals' – by which Hitler means the Marxist and Socialist protagonists of the 1918 revolution – the broad implications of a National Socialist seizure of power are clear. Here, and elsewhere, Hitler refers to 'hanging' little criminals, in a manner which makes it obvious that he thinks the same punishment should be meted out to the 'big' criminals i.e. the leaders of the 1918 revolution; similarly, the reference to 'execution' is hardly ambiguous. Neither are these isolated moments of polemical excess. Elsewhere, Hitler insists that in 1914 the German parliament should have been 'brought to its senses, with bayonets if necessary'; 'if the best men were dying at the front, the least we could do was to wipe out this vermin' (MK, 155). Such comments reflect his view that the anti-war lobby in the Social Democratic parliamentary group, which grew in size and influence as the war progressed, played a crucial role in undermining Germany's ability to fight. His hostility to everything the left stood for was compounded by his belief that the Social Democrats had betrayed the troops at the front in 1918. In a passage of radical invective against the 'November criminals' in his *Second Book* Hitler calls for a 'merciless war against the infernal defilers of German honour', claiming that 'I could reconcile myself to any of the former enemy, but . . . my hatred against the betrayers of our own

people in our own ranks is and remains irreconcilable' (2B, 116).★
The implications of such language are quite easy to discern.

Similarly, the language of violence in the second passage
quoted above is anything but accidental. 'Destroy', 'destruction', 'extermination' – these goals are to be pursued 'in ruthless
attack'. This is the typical language of a text which resonates
with constant use of terms such as 'eradication', 'elimination',
'annihilation', and which calls for their implementation in 'merciless', 'pitiless' and 'brutal' fashion. These, together with Hitler's
repeated rejection of 'half measures', and his scornful criticisms
of 'false sentimentality' or misguided humanitarianism, create
the cumulative sense of a politician whose vision is not only one
of extreme violence, but of potentially murderous consequences.

In conclusion, as well as thinking about the political significance of the genre of Hitler's texts, we need to think
about the nature and connotations of the language itself.
Examination of the ways in which military analogies and
metaphors operate in the text suggests that one key to
understanding Hitler's work lies in recognizing how profound the impact of the First World War was on his thinking
and, by extension, on the political culture of inter-war
Germany. However, the images of military violence that permeate his writing are not merely *symptomatic* of a broader
war-induced cultural crisis: they are also *programmatic*,
embodying a clear threat of extreme brutality towards those
seen as Germany's enemies. Many of the anti-Semitic images
in Hitler's writings can be found in, say, the work of Houston
Stewart Chamberlain. Yet when reading Chamberlain's work
we hardly sense that we are dealing with an advocate of

---

★ I have used the 1961 translation here; the page reference refers to that
edition.

murder. When reading Hitler, by contrast, we often do — even before we have considered the detail of what he is discussing. This is because the message is not only to be found in the arguments of the text, but is embedded in the language itself.

# 4

## HISTORY

If consideration of the literary forms and linguistic motifs of Hitler's work reveal him as a self-appointed man of destiny and a man of extreme violence, we still need to explain how it was that Hitler came to focus his destructive ambitions in the way that he did. Why, specifically, did the Jews become the object of his hatred? Why was genocide the eventual outcome of this hatred? Most immediately, the answer to this lies in Hitler's explanation of the causes of Germany's defeat in the First World War. However, it is important to recognize that he regarded these as only surface manifestations of a deeper problem. The nature of Hitler's anti-Semitism and its significance can only be explored once one has appreciated his reading of Germany's development in the nineteenth century. The starting point for an exploration of his hatred of the Jews, then, lies in a consideration of his views of history, and this chapter will briefly explore these.

Consider these passages:

a) Politics is history in the making. History itself represents the progression of a people's struggle for existence. I use the phrase 'struggle for existence' intentionally here, because in reality that struggle for daily bread, whether in peace or war, is a never-ending battle against thousands and thousands of obstacles, just as life itself is an eternal struggle against death. For human beings know no more than any other creature in the world why they live, but life is filled with the longing to preserve it. The most primitive creature knows only the instinct of the self-preservation of its own 'I'; for higher beings this carries over to wife and child, and for those higher still to the entire species. But when man – not infrequently, it seems – renounces his own self-preservation instinct for the benefit of the species, he is still doing it the highest service. Because not infrequently it is this renunciation of the individual that grants life to the collective whole, and thus yet again to the individual. Hence the sudden courage of the mother defending her young and the heroism of the man protecting his people. The magnitude of the self-preservation instinct corresponds to the two most powerful motivations in life: hunger and love. While the satisfaction of eternal hunger guarantees self-preservation, the gratification of love assures its furtherance. In truth these two drives are the rulers of life. And even if the fleshless aesthete protests against such a claim a thousand times, the fact of his own existence already refutes his protest. Whatever is made of flesh and blood can never escape the laws which determined its coming into being. [. . .]

(2B, 7–8)


b) [T]he regulation of the relationship between the population and the land area is of the utmost importance for the existence of a people. Yes, one can say for the sake of expedience that a people's entire struggle for survival in reality consists only of securing the necessary territory and land as a general precondition for feeding the growing population. Since the population continues to grow while the territory and land itself remains the same, tensions must gradually appear which at first find expression in shortage, that can be counterbalanced for a certain time by greater industriousness, more ingenious production methods or special thriftiness, but which one day can no longer be overcome by all these means. The leaders of the people's struggle for survival then have the duty thoroughly to eliminate this unbearable relationship – in other words, to re-establish an acceptable ratio between population and land area.

Now, in the life of a people there are several ways to correct the imbalance between population and land area. The most natural is the adaptation of the territory from time to time to fit the increased population. This requires a determination to fight and the risk of bloodshed. But this very bloodshed is also the only one that can be justified to a people.

(2B, 18)

Before exploring the implications of these ideas it is worth pausing to reflect upon their influences. Several central tenets of nineteenth-century thought collide in these arguments, which contain little, if anything, that one might consider original to Hitler. As we have already seen, the fascination with notions of race can be traced back at least as far as Gobineau. The interest in history as the study of the rise and fall of civilizations, and (elsewhere) the attribution of specific positive or negative cultural characteristics to different nations or races, recalls the writings of the amateur historian-cum-anthropologist Houston

Stewart Chamberlain. The belief that both different species and individual members of a species exist in a state of permanent struggle for survival, with the stronger emerging triumphant and the weak going under, is an obvious example of the way in which the ideas of Charles Darwin permeated the late nineteenth- and early twentieth-century world. Moreover, Hitler's belief that history was governed by fundamental, immutable laws not only offers an interesting parallel to the writings of Karl Marx, but reflects the 'spirit of science' that increasingly pervaded almost all spheres of intellectual life as the nineteenth century wore on.

Where did Hitler get his ideas from? We are quite well informed about at least some of his reading habits. Ernst Hanfstaengl, a wealthy early associate and benefactor of the future *Führer* during his Munich years, tells us in his memoirs that Hitler was a 'voracious' reader who read widely on Frederick the Great, the French Revolution and Napoleon; he also constantly referred to Clausewitz, 'whom he could quote by the yard'. For the rest, Hanfstaengl informs us that Hitler owned histories of the First World War by Hermann Stegemann and Erich Ludendorff, and general histories of Germany by Einhardt and Heinrich von Treitschke. He also owned a nineteenth-century illustrated encyclopaedia, a collection of heroic myths and other First World War memoirs. Hans Frank – his co-insurgent at the Munich putsch, fellow inmate in Landsberg prison and later Governor-General of occupied Poland – also tells us in his memoirs that Hitler read widely during the period of incarceration in which he wrote *Mein Kampf*: Nietzsche, Ranke, and again Treitschke and Houston Stewart Chamberlain. In Munich Hitler also heard lectures by the prominent historian Professor Karl Alexander von Müller, and through his acquaintance with

Rudolf Hess was introduced to the geopolitical theories of Karl Haushofer.

One can certainly detect echoes of the ideas of various nineteenth- and early twentieth-century writers, politicians and philosophers in much of what Hitler wrote. However, these echoes are always vague and half-comprehended, and hardly constitute grounds for considering Hitler's thought inside of the traditions of 'intellectual history' as it is conventionally understood. Hitler did not read with the open mind of the intellectual, but for confirmation of what he already believed. He was not interested in the 'life of the mind', or in ideas for their own sake. Instead, he sought through his reading to lend legitimacy to his prejudices and thereby to invest them with the aura of philosophical profundity.

Rather than take these unmistakable references and echoes as evidence that we should see in Hitler's writings the expressions of an intellectual political philosopher at work, therefore, we should see them more generally in fact as examples of the vulgarization of key elements of the scientific, historical, and philosophical traditions of the nineteenth and early twentieth century. This vulgarization occurred partly through acquaintance with the relevant canonical texts of political philosophy themselves, but partly too through the second-hand acquisition of knowledge from pamphlets, newspapers, lectures and conversations. The resultant thoughts were mixed, in turn, with ideas derived from the reading of second-rate popular volumes which themselves had no scholarly or historical value. Some of this largely spurious knowledge was picked up during Hitler's time in Vienna, some of it during the First World War and some of it afterwards – it is not always possible to know for sure precisely when Hitler was exposed to any given set of ideas or writings for the first time. The point is that one

can perfectly easily connect Hitler to the world of thought of
the nineteenth and early twentieth centuries without falsely
ascribing to him the status of a thinker or philosopher on the
level of Darwin, for example.

What of the ideas in the quoted passages themselves? As
these demonstrate, a vulgarized form of Darwinist thinking
was central to Hitler's world-view. For Hitler, struggle was not
only the unifying motif of his own life, it was the dominant
motive force of history. For all the religious analogies and
metaphors that permeate his writing – such as his use of the
language of providence, already noted – it is clear from this
passage that this struggle, the expression of the fundamental
'instinct for self-preservation', contains the only meaning of
existence. Hitler believed that human beings were driven by
two fundamental urges: the urge to satisfy hunger and the
urge to procreate. There was no meaning to the universe outside the satisfaction of these biological needs, which were
ends in themselves.

The same biological urges that characterized the struggle of
the individual, moreover, applied to peoples and nations, or
races, as a whole. Nations, or races, lived out their existence in
a permanent struggle for self-perpetuation, expressed again in
the constant search for food and the constant urge for biological regeneration. Importantly, as this passage makes clear, when
the essential interests of the nation as a whole are at stake, the
needs of the individual are subordinate to the greater needs of
the community. The relationship of the individual to the
human community was essentially governed by the same basic
rules as those that controlled the animal kingdom: the higher
interests of the species ranked above the right to life of the
individual. This is worth noting because it underlines the key
point that the totalitarian practices of the Nazi Party once it was

in power were rooted not only in the desire to suppress brutally all political opposition but in the fundamental belief that the interests of the individual must be ruthlessly subordinated to the needs of the community if the nation itself was to survive.

If struggle was an eternal law, space was limited: the Earth, after all, has a finite surface. The nation's search for food, expressed as a constant struggle for land, would thus inevitably lead to war with other nations. Wars were the natural expression of the eternal struggle for space. In this struggle for the living space necessary to guarantee an adequate supply of food there was only one law: the strong would survive and the weak would perish. It was a struggle fought without mercy. The model for this, again, was the animal world. Humans had obligations to their own race but none to others, just as 'you will never find a fox who in his inner attitude might, for example, show humanitarian tendencies towards geese, as similarly there is no cat with a friendly inclination towards mice' (MK, 259).

Nations thus existed in a constant Darwinian struggle for survival against one another. They had no moral right to land – for Hitler, might was right, and the only space to which any people were entitled was that which they could defend. In his view, 'soil exists for the people which possesses the force to take it and the industry to cultivate it' (MK,123). Accordingly, a nation's borders were never natural or fixed, but transitory expressions of the state of play in the eternal struggle for land and food. As a people grew in strength, so its needs grew, which would inevitably lead to the expansion of its borders; by the same token, 'declining' races would see their borders contract.

The constant search for food would not always manifest itself immediately in the outbreak of war. In the short term, there were several alternatives. Firstly, a people could satisfy its increased need for food by more efficient cultivation of the land that it already possessed. This, however, had its limits. Hitler regarded it as empirically observable that people's demands for consumption grew as time went by. More intensive cultivation of existing soil could satisfy the increased consumption needs of an existing population but it could not meet the growing needs of a population that was also expanding: sooner or later, the nation would have to pursue additional living space.

Alternatively, a nation could seek to satisfy its needs through trade. This, however, was also only a temporary possibility, which could postpone but not prevent the inevitable recourse to war. All nations were engaged in a similar bid to improve their living standards through increased trade, but the world market for exports was not endless, placing limits on how far this strategy could be pursued. Overseas colonies were too small to provide sufficient extra space or resources to satisfy the needs of the colonizing power's people; in any case, competition for markets would itself inevitably bring nations into conflict with one another. War would sooner or later occur. For these reasons, Hitler believed that the *Weltpolitik* of the late nineteenth century had been based on fundamentally flawed premises. Trade-based pursuit of a country's vital needs also had other very detrimental effects: in stimulating industry, it led to increased urbanization, and it also fostered the dangerous illusion that a people's essential needs could be satisfied in the long term through peaceful means. It thus reduced their ability to fight, placing them at a disastrous disadvantage when such a need arose.

The only other alternative was by far the worst: instead of expanding its space to bring it back into line with its growth in size, thus restoring a healthy balance between a people and its soil, a nation could *reduce* the size of its population in order to fit into the limited available space. This could occur either through emigration – Hitler explained the nineteenth-century wave of European migration to America in these terms – or it could occur through birth control. Both, however, were unacceptable since they condemned the race as a whole to decline. Emigration, Hitler observed, always led to the loss of the most healthy, able members of a race, leaving the inferior ones behind. Birth control, for Hitler, was even worse, because it ran counter to the fundamental laws of nature.

For Hitler, birth control should not be practised by humans, but left to nature itself. Natural selection ensured the survival of the fittest, sparing 'the few healthiest and most robust in the struggle for survival' (2B, 21), whereas modern methods of birth control led to the complete opposite. Many potentially healthy members of the race were withheld from the community by selfish parents who placed their own interests above the essential needs of the nation. Meanwhile, misguided humanitarianism ('our current, dishonest sentimental bourgeois-patriotic nonsense' [2B, 21]) ensured that endless time and effort was spent keeping alive weak, inferior children who were of no use to the race. The model, for Hitler, was Sparta, whose practice of sparing only the strongest babies was such that it must be regarded as 'the first racial state'. Birth control, by contrast, led inevitably to a decline in the health of the race as a whole.

This, of course, was unacceptable to Hitler: in the eternal struggle for existence waged between nations, who survived and who perished was determined by the health of the race. Healthy races triumphed, weak ones went under. What constituted a healthy race? For Hitler the answer was simple: a homogeneous one.

Hitler's views on history boil down to a crude, simplistic version of Social Darwinism whose essential features can be summarized in a few paragraphs. However, understanding his views on the general principles of history – on life as struggle, on the survival of the fittest and on the eternal competition between races – and, most importantly, recognizing that his belief that success or failure in the eternal struggle for space depended not on superficial issues such as military strategy or the relative size of armies and navies but rested instead on the underlying health of the races involved in the struggle is crucial. Not only does it enable us to see how central to his world-view the principle of 'struggle' was: it also enables us to understand more fully his explanations of why it was that Germany lost the First World War, and what the necessary remedies should be. When considering Hitler's analysis of the causes of Germany's defeat in 1918 it is important to remember that he regarded military developments on the battlefield, the evolution of the fighting capacities and morale of the German army, and political developments on the German home front as mere epiphenomena, surface expressions of an underlying process of racial decline which meant that Germany had been unable to protect herself in the struggle for existence. Understanding the underlying nature of the ills which Hitler believed were affecting the German nation is essential if we are to explain how he imagined the solution that he did. Before considering the nature of Hitler's antidote to the nation's ills, however – and why he focused his hatred on the Jews – we still need to consider his views on the First World War, the German defeat and the revolution of 1918 in greater detail.

# 5

# WAR, REVOLUTION AND NATIONAL REBIRTH

a) To me those hours seemed like a release from the painful feelings of my youth. Even today I am not ashamed to say that, overpowered by stormy enthusiasm, I fell down on my knees and thanked Heaven from an overflowing heart for granting me the good fortune of being permitted to live at this time.

A fight for freedom had begun, mightier than the Earth had ever seen; for once Destiny had begun its course, the conviction dawned on even the broad masses that this time not the fate of Serbia or Austria was involved, but whether the German nation was to be or not to be.

(MK, 148)

b) But, while those at the front were undertaking the last preparations for the final conclusion of the eternal struggle, while endless transports of men and matériel were rolling towards the West Front, and the troops were being trained for the great attack – the biggest piece of chicanery in the whole war broke out in Germany.

Germany must not be victorious; in the last hour, with

victory already threatening to be with the German banners, a means was chosen which seemed suited to stifle the German spring attack in the germ with one blow, to make victory impossible:

The munitions strike was organized.

If it succeeded, the German front was bound to collapse, and the *Vorwärts* desire that this time victory should not be with the German banners would inevitably be fulfilled. Owing to the lack of munitions, the front would inevitably be pierced in a few weeks; thus the offensive was thwarted, the Entente saved, international capital was made master of Germany, and the inner aim of the Marxist swindle of nations achieved.

To smash the national economy and establish the rule of international capital – a goal which actually was achieved, thanks to the stupidity and credulity of the one side and the bottomless cowardice of the other.

To be sure, the munitions strike did not have all the hoped-for success with regard to starving the front of arms; it collapsed too soon for the lack of munitions as such – as the plan had been – to doom the army to destruction.

But how much more terrible was the moral damage that had been done!

In the first place: what was the army fighting for if the homeland itself no longer wanted victory? For whom the immense sacrifices and privations? The soldier is expected to fight for victory and the homeland goes on strike against it!

(MK, 177)

The moment of imagined national unity in 1914 celebrated in later right-wing mythology was not confined to the troops marching to the front. For the nationalist right, the outbreak of the First World War marked a moment when all the social and political divisions from which Germany had suffered were suspended. Instead, the people rallied around the Kaiser, whose proclamation that 'I know no parties, only Germans' symbolized the 'Burgfrieden', or 'peace in the citadel' by which all German parties were to abide for the length of the war. As ever, Hitler rewrites history in the language of his own Manichaean world-view, and recasts the memory of August 1914 in the light of his subsequent wartime experiences. The wave of patriotism which swept 'the broad masses', such as it was, was not born of a general welcome that the struggle 'to be or not to be' had finally broken out – few predicted the four years of slaughter that were to follow – but was informed by the widespread sense that the war would be over by Christmas.

All was not well, however. Under the pressure of war, the national consensus broke down. As the burdens placed by the war on the masses grew, discontent at its continued prosecution set in and pressure for a negotiated peace increased. This was especially true of the left, whose 'peace wing' constantly grew. The German parliament passed the famous 'Peace Resolution' in July 1917; morale on the home front declined; there were demonstrations and strikes in the cities, including the Berlin munitions strike of January 1918 to which Hitler refers; finally the revolution, which brought monarchical rule to an end in Germany, broke out in November 1918 at a time when, crucially, the German armies were still on French soil.

For broad sections of the German right, defeat in the war was blamed on the collapse of the home front. They believed that Germany's armies had remained undefeated in the field, but that left-wing agitators – *Vorwärts* was the main newspaper of the Social Democratic Party – had undermined national unity and forced revolution on the country in an act of unspeakable treachery. It was the civilian politicians of the left who had signed the 'armistice'. It was the democratic government set up in the wake of war that had signed the Treaty of Versailles, and with it the hated 'War Guilt Clause', which in Hitler's eyes put the blame firmly on the shoulders of the left-wing parties who had come to power in 1918.

The truth, of course, was completely different. With the failure of the German spring offensive of 1918, her armies were in a hopeless position, and her soldiers were deserting in their thousands. Her leading generals had recognized the hopelessness of the position, and had ceded power to the civilian government in order to force it to bear the political burden of signing the armistice. But this is not the point: the point is that broad sectors of the German right interpreted the experiences of 1918 in this way, and framed their 'solutions' accordingly.

Hitler accepted the German right's critique of the 'November criminals' who had 'stabbed Germany in the back' while her armies fought in the field, stating that 'for four and a half years the German army organization resisted the largest enemy coalition of all time. The civilian, democratic, decomposed inner leadership broke down literally at the first blow from a few hundred rabble and deserters' (2B, 36). But whereas for many on the right the activities of unpatriotic left-wing agitators during the war provided sufficient explanation in itself for the German defeat, for Hitler this was only a symptom of deeper causes. Despite the moment of unity in 1914, he argued, 'in the long peace of the pre-War years, certain harmful features had appeared and had been recognized as such, though next to nothing was done against their virus [. . .]' (MK, 212); as a result 'we more than deserved this defeat. It is only the greatest outward symptom of decay amid a whole series of inner symptoms' (MK, 209). In other words, Germany had gone to war weakened by internal problems and divisions that had fatally undermined her capacity to resist and had thus made defeat inevitable. These problems were, again, merely surface manifestations of a deeper malaise whose explanation lay in an understanding of the laws of history.

What, then, were the underlying causes of Germany's 1918 collapse? Hitler argued that the nineteenth century's one-sided emphasis on commerce and international trade had led to an unwelcome transfer of property ownership to 'stock exchange capital', and to a weakening of the peasant class in favour of the urban working class. The commercial imperatives of the bourgeois age had fostered a spirit of extreme selfishness, moreover, and a belief that economic activity merely served the interests of the individual entrepreneur, not those of the nation as a whole. As a result, the justified needs of the urban working class were neglected, and social inequalities grew. The workers in the cities, living as they did in appalling conditions (described by Hitler at length in *Mein Kampf* in sketches of life in pre-war Vienna), became alienated from the nation and increasingly susceptible to the siren attractions of Marxism. This belief-system, with its message of human equality, internationalism and pacifism, had eroded the workers' willingness to fight, as had the press, which had systematically fostered false belief in the possibility of endless peaceful human progress. A large part of the population was uncommitted to the essential needs of the nation. Germany had thus gone to war fatally weakened by her internal divisions and her unpreparedness to fight.

Who, for Hitler, were the main beneficiaries of the stock exchange? The Jews. Who were the main owners of the press?

The Jews. Who was responsible for the spread of Marxism, and whose interests did Marxism serve? The Jews. According to Hitler, Marxism and pacifism were tools for sowing social division and undermining Germany's ability to fight, leading to the destruction of the German nation and paving the way for the triumph of an international Jewish conspiracy. Behind all the negative political developments on the home front stood Germany's great racial enemies, the Jews, acting as 'wirepullers' in a revolution for which they had long been preparing the ground.

The beneficiaries of the revolution were the 'international stock-exchange Jews': in claiming that 'international capital' had been made 'master of Germany', Hitler is most likely referring to the reparations clauses of the Treaty of Versailles, or to the Dawes Plan of 1924 which rescheduled reparations payments just as Hitler was beginning to write his book.

Everything thus fitted into a simplistic, overarching explanation: *behind everything stood the Jews.* For Hitler, the Jews were a separate race. They were unique among races, however, in that unlike all others they did not have their own territory to defend. They were an international race. In the eternal history of racial struggle they thus played a peculiar role. With no living space of their own, they were obliged to live a parasitical existence. This they had been doing in Germany for some time: hence the underlying weakness of the German nation and her defeat in war. Above all, the Jews had been using Marxism to weaken the German nation from within, bringing it to the point at which the international Jewish conspiracy could triumph.

According to Hitler's own account, he came to recognize the supposed links between the Jews, Social Democracy and

Marxism during his years in Vienna. It is in his description of this period that he claims that: 'Meanwhile, I had learned to understand the connection between this doctrine of destruction and the nature of a people of which, up to that time, I had known next to nothing' (MK, 47). Here, too, he observes that: 'When I recognized the Jew as the leader of Social Democracy, the scales dropped from my eyes' (MK, 56). In his chapter on 'general political considerations based on my Vienna period' he also claims that: 'I do not know what my attitude towards the Jews, Social Democracy, or rather Marxism as a whole, the social question, etc., would be today if at such an early time the pressure of destiny – and my own study – had not built up a basic stock of personal opinions within me' (MK, 114–5).

The repeated insistence by Hitler that he came to see the links between Marxism and the Jews as early as this should be treated with some scepticism, however. Relatively few of Hitler's immediate post-war utterances make this link, suggesting that it formed in his mind only later. If anything, it was the link between international capitalism and the Jews that was stronger in Hitler's mind until the mid-1920s; it was only around the time when he wrote *Mein Kampf* that the connection with Marxism was firmly established in his consciousness. The insistence that he recognized a link even before the First World War would seem, therefore, to be part of Hitler's attempt to rewrite his life as that of the man of destiny and unshakeable conviction: the fact that he asserted this so repeatedly in *Mein Kampf* does, however, underline how central to Hitler's world-view this concept had become by the time it was written.

If we are to believe Hitler, he initially blamed the supporters themselves for their unpatriotic stance. His descriptions of encounters with Viennese Social Democratic workers recall his deep frustration with those fellow Germans who believed that the nation was an invention of the capitalist classes and saw 'the fatherland as an instrument of the bourgeoisie for the exploitation of the working class' (MK, 37). Eventually, however, he came to distinguish between the mass of the German workers, whom he regarded as fundamentally decent, and the agitation of the Social Democratic, Marxist leadership. Having immersed himself in the literature of the left in order to understand better its attractions, he revised his view: 'Only a fool can behold the work of this villainous poisoner and still condemn the victim' (MK, 39).

Crucially, however, Hitler did not only blame the left. His assertion in the passage above that the Marxists' goal was achieved 'thanks to the stupidity and credulity of the one side and the bottomless cowardice of the other' reminds us again that Hitler's criticisms were directed not only against Social Democracy but also against the forces of the 'old right', the 'upper ten thousand' whose failure to solve 'the social problem' had made it possible for Marxism, and thus for the Jews, to spread their pernicious influence.

The precondition for any national revival, therefore, lay in rectifying these problems:

> The great domestic task of the future lies in the elimination of these general symptoms of the decay of our people. This is the mission of the National Socialist movement. A new body-politic must arise from this work which overcomes even the worst disadvantage of the present, the cleavage between the classes, for which the bourgeoisie and Marxism are equally guilty.
>
> The aim of this domestic political reform work must ultimately be the regaining of our people's strength for the

prosecution of its struggle for existence and thereby the
strength to represent its vital interests abroad.

(2B, 79)*

In general terms, it is not difficult to interpret this passage, but
the precise shape of the new nation which Hitler envisaged
emerging – the so-called 'People's Community', or *Volksgemeinschaft* – is harder to discern, either in these lines or in any other.
By 'eliminating symptoms of decay' Hitler is simultaneously
referring to two things. Firstly, as the immediate context of
the passage from which this extract is taken suggests, the negative
racial influences of the Jews must be removed, as must the political influences of internationalism, democracy and pacifism. The
exact manner in which these elements are to be removed is
unclear, but given what we know about the violent proclivities
of Hitler the outlines of what a National Socialist seizure of
power portends for its opponents are obvious. It is equally clear,
by extension, that the new Germany would be nationalistic,
authoritarian and militaristic.

Second, overcoming these symptoms involves tackling the
'social problem'. Again, what this means in the detail is very
hard to read. Given what Hitler argued about the inequalities
of the nineteenth century and the selfishness of the commercial bourgeoisie, we can surmise that the worst excesses of
social inequality are to be overcome in the new National
Socialist Germany and that the workers are to be reintegrated
into the nation; the notions of 'community' which he advocated also contain more than a sense that the economy will be
run not only in the interests of the individual but for the

---

* I have used a modified version of the 1961 translation here. The page
reference refers to that edition.

greater good of the nation. Yet it is also clear in this passage that the 'socialism' implicit in the vision of community being espoused here is not one in which property is to be national- ized and taken under state control: Hitler is advocating the end of the 'cleavage between the classes', not the abolition of the classes themselves. In other words, in place of a society divided along class lines, Hitler envisaged an egalitarian, organicist community of Germans in which the economy was managed for the common good of the nation and in which individual Germans worked for the good of the com- munity as a whole.

This, however, was not an end in itself. Eradicating Germany's internal enemies and overcoming her internal divi- sions was part of a broader process of national renewal. Winning over the working class was essential because 'it is numerically the stronger and above all comprises all those elements without which a national resurrection is unthinkable and impossible' (MK, 301), Hitler argued – the solution of the 'social problem' was thus the prelude to a broader process of national rebirth. Domestic reform would lead to a removal of the negative pacifist influences of the past and to a rediscovery of the ability to fight: in other words, it was the precondition for the renewed pursuit of living space. Unlike in the First World War, however, the presence of a homogeneous, united 'people's community' ready to fight would ensure that in the next stage of the eternal struggle for existence the Germans would emerge victorious. Again, it is this emphasis on 'resur- rection' and rebirth, on the necessity to regain strength which has been temporarily lost to the nation because of certain negative influences, strength which can be recovered if the will and determination are there, that marks Hitler out as a fascist thinker.

In summary: we have seen how, in various ways, Hitler was inspired by the First World War. Yet consideration of what he has to say about events on the home front and the origins of the revolution of 1918 reveal something else: he was also haunted by it. For Hitler, the German armies had been stabbed in the back by the treacherous forces of Marxism. These, in turn, were acting in the interests of a Jewish world conspiracy, the final aim of which was the destruction of the German nation. That the Jews had been able to gain such a strong influence among the German working class was due to the failure of the old elites to address the 'social problem'. In order to restore Germany's fortunes, therefore, Hitler demanded the creation of a 'people's community': an egalitarian community of all Germans in which class divisions had been overcome and the workers had been reconciled to the nation. Only when such a community had been forged could Germany go to war again in the pursuit of her vital interests without fear of the internal collapse she had suffered in 1918.

Implicit in this vision of a 'people's community', then, was the idea that Germany's enemies, the Marxists and the Jews, would have to be removed and their pernicious influence eradicated. Hitler's description of them as 'revolutionary pyromaniac murderers, plunderers of the people and traitors to the nation' (MK, 493) and his demands, noted in a previous chapter, that the 'November criminals' should be 'executed' leave us in little doubt that these adversaries were to meet a violent end.

Would the purging of the German nation and the creation of the 'people's community' necessarily demand genocide, however? In passing, we have noted Hitler's habit of referring to Germany's problems in terms of 'illness' or 'decay', with the influence of the Jews being described as 'poison' or a 'virus'. Indeed, slow and careful reading of *Mein Kampf* and the *Second Book* reveals that his writing is replete not just with military metaphors and analogies but with biological and medical ones as well. As we shall see in the next chapter, this biological and medical language offers the key to recognizing the implicitly genocidal message that resonates through Hitler's work.

## 6

# THE JEWS

The offices were filled with Jews. Nearly every clerk was a Jew and nearly every Jew was a clerk. I was amazed at this plethora of warriors of the chosen people and could not help but compare them with their rare representatives at the front.

As regards economic life, things were even worse. Here the Jews had become really 'indispensable'. The spider was slowly beginning to suck the blood out of the people's pores. Through the war corporations, they had found an instrument with which, little by little, to finish off the national free economy.

The necessity of an unlimited centralization was emphasized.

Thus, in the year 1916–17 nearly the whole of production was under the control of Jewish finance.

(MK, 175)

This passage, in which Hitler describes a leave visit to the home front during the First World War, is typical of the crude anti-Semitic invective that characterizes much of *Mein Kampf*.

Many of the sections in which Hitler discusses or refers to the
Jews merely replicate, albeit in particularly nauseating fashion,
the standard anti-Semitic rhetoric of the time. This, in turn,
often drew on images of Jews present in Western culture for
centuries. Other passages reproduce traditional stereotypes
modified to suit the specific circumstances of the First World
War. Here, for example, we are informed that the offices of
the home front are filled with Jews. The implication – which
reflects a widespread charge levelled by the nationalist and
racist right during the war – is that Jews were not 'doing
their bit' at the front. While brave Germans fought and died
for the fatherland, Jewish cowards shirked their duty, enjoying
the protection of cosy office jobs. There was, it should be
emphasized, no truth in this at all. Nearly 100,000 Jews
fought in the German army in the First World War, and
12,000 were killed. Secondly, and very clearly, the charge of
'war-profiteering' is being laid. Again, this was a standard
complaint of the German right. As baseless as the first accu-
sation, it reflects the widespread search for a scapegoat for the
inadequacies of the German munitions industries, for the food
shortages which were already growing acute by the middle of
the war, and for growing inflation.

The charge of 'war-profiteering' did not itself, of course,
exist in isolation, and drew its rhetorical force from its
connections with much older refrains in the anti-Semitic
traditions of Germany. Throughout Hitler's writing, the
Jews are associated with the malign, exploitative forces of
capitalism. Not only were they associated with the evils of the
'international stock exchange', as we have already seen, they
were also blamed for the negative impact of the department
stores on small German shopkeepers (in the *Second Book*, for
example, Hitler refers to 'department-store Jewesses' [2B, 31]),

and were generally characterized by Hitler as being obsessed
with money to the point where 'cheating' and 'swindling'
(favourite terms) were second nature to them.

Neither were Jews to blame only for the negative effects of
capitalism on the German nation – they were, for Hitler,
responsible for all the negative manifestations of modern
urban life. They were linked to the press ('the pack of Jewish
press hounds'); they were characterized as carping cultural
critics (here we may detect an echo of Hitler's frustration at
the world's failure to appreciate his artistic talents); they were
seen as the agents of decadent modern theatre, modern art,
and modern literature – all of which Hitler regarded as
licentious and pornographic, and corrosive of healthy traditional values.

The castigation of allegedly Jewish modern culture for its
depravity draws our attention to another aspect of Hitler's
anti-Semitism, one which drew on older stereotypes but was
also closely linked to his biological world-view: it manifests
itself as an expression of sexual – or sometimes sexualized –
neuroses concerning the 'purity' of the nation and specifically
that of its women. The Jews, we learn, are responsible for
prostitution (unsurprisingly, since this reflects the 'mammonization of our mating instinct', according to *Mein Kampf*).
Similarly, Jews are depicted as lustful despoilers, seducing
innocent German girls, 'defiling' them, and thus undermining
the purity of their blood and that of the nation as a whole.
Again, this image of the Jew as sexual predator was not an
invention of Hitler's, nor even of the modern era: it was
already centuries old.

Our consideration of the passage that opened this chapter
is not exhausted, however, if we take from it only the recog-
nition that much of Hitler's anti-Semitic rhetoric is couched

in the language of traditional prejudice or contemporary political scapegoating. The striking image of the spider sucking the blood out of the people's pores is typical of another central feature of his descriptions of Jews, namely his regular habit of resorting to crude, and often lurid, animal imagery. We have already seen supposedly Jewish journalists described as 'yelping hounds'; elsewhere, these journalists are described as 'trufflers'; at various points in the two books we similarly find Jews referred to as 'octopuses', 'vipers' or 'serpents'.

The rhetorical effect that Hitler sought to create in his use of such imagery is not hard to discern: in depicting the Jews as animals traditionally associated with characteristics such as stealth, slyness, or cunning, and in using images of animals that ensnare or slowly ingest their victims, creeping up on them unnoticed until it is too late, Hitler conjured up the crude vision of a Germany slowly, inexorably being taken over by the Jewish world conspiracy. But the constant use of such animal imagery is not simply indicative of Hitler's limited repertoire of metaphors and analogies: it reflects his fundamental belief in the biological nature of the struggle between nations. Furthermore, as the repeated use of the image of the viper suggests, Hitler did not just believe that the German nation was being hunted or ensnared: he believed that it was being poisoned. This brings us to the most important metaphor at work in *Mein Kampf*, and the one which is key to understanding its genocidal implications: that of the nation as a human body:

> Since the Jew never possessed a state with definite territorial limits and therefore never called a culture his own, the conception arose that this was a people which should be reckoned among the ranks of the *nomads*. This is a fallacy

as great as it is dangerous . . . No, the Jew is no nomad; for the nomad had also a definite attitude towards the concept of work which could serve as a basis for his later development in so far as the necessary intellectual premises were present. In him the basic idealistic view is present, even if in infinite dilution, hence in his whole being he may seem strange to the Aryan peoples, but not unattractive. In the Jew, however, this attitude is not at all present; for that reason he was never a nomad, but only and always a *parasite* in the body of other peoples. That he sometimes left his previous living space has nothing to do with his own purpose, but results from the fact that from time to time he was thrown out by the host nations he had misused. His spreading is a typical phenomenon for all parasites; he always seeks a new feeding ground for his race.

This, however, has nothing to do with nomadism, for the reason that a Jew never thinks of leaving a territory that he has occupied, but remains where he is, and he sits so fast that even by force it is very hard to drive him out. His extension to ever-new countries occurs only in the moment in which certain conditions for his existence are there present, without which – unlike the nomad – he would not change his residence. He is and remains the typical parasite, a sponger who like a noxious bacillus keeps spreading as soon as a favourable medium invites him. And the effect of his existence is also like that of spongers: wherever he appears, the host people dies out after a shorter or longer period.

Thus the Jew of all times has lived in the states of other peoples, and there formed his own state, which, to be sure, habitually sailed under the disguise of 'religious community' as long as outward circumstances made a complete

revelation of his nature seem inadvisable. But as soon as
he felt strong enough to do without the protective cloak, he
always dropped the veil and suddenly became what so
many of the others previously did not want to believe and
see: the Jew.

(MK, 275–7)

As this passage again demonstrates, Hitler did not regard Jews
as Germans: he regarded them as a separate race. This was not
an accidental or passing observation: it was central to Hitler's
understanding of his own anti-Semitism in relation to that of
previous generations and of others; the passage therefore oper-
ates, like many others, as an act of self-definition against
competitors on the right of German politics. In rejecting the
claim that the Jews should be seen merely as a religious community – like Protestants or Catholics – Hitler is rejecting the
possibility of assimilation, and with it the rhetoric of much
nineteenth-century anti-Semitism.

For many nineteenth-century anti-Semites, especially liberals who saw in religion an expression of irrational
superstition, the 'Jewish problem' lay in the offending presence of those who claimed the right to cultural difference: the
universalist aspirations of liberal politicians were incompatible
with the presence of people who wanted to perpetuate religious or cultural distinctiveness. For liberals, therefore, the
solution to the 'Jewish problem' lay in the Jews renouncing
their Jewishness: if the Jews would only convert to the ways
and beliefs of the Christian majority the issue would go away
of its own accord.

For Hitler, of course, such a position was absurd and the
'solution' was a logical impossibility. A Jew could no more
become a German than a dog could become a cat. For him,

religious or cultural anti-Semitism was pointless, as it missed the central issue and hence was doomed to be ineffectual. In *Mein Kampf* he informs us that: 'It is obvious that combating Jewry on such a basis could provide the Jews with small cause for concern. If the worst came to the worst, a small splash of baptismal water could always save the business and the Jew at the same time' (MK, 110). Worse than this, however, religious anti-Semitism or the successful pursuit of conversion to Christianity brought new dangers, as it deluded ordinary people into thinking that the problem had been solved: 'It was a sham anti-Semitism which was almost worse than none at all; for it lulled people into security; they thought they had the foe by the ears, while in reality they themselves were being led by the nose' (MK, 110).

Recognizing the reasoning behind Hitler's rejection of the possibility of Jewish assimilation is crucial if we are to grasp what distinguished his brand of anti-Semitism from pre-existing prejudices, and essential if we are to understand why genocide was a logical possibility within his system of thought. For all Hitler's tendency to couch his anti-Semitic attacks in traditional forms or to resort to longstanding images and rhetoric, his anti-Semitism was fundamentally different both from pre-modern forms of anti-Semitism and from most nineteenth-century expressions of this prejudice. Above all, Hitler believed that his anti-Semitism was *scientific*, and rooted in the laws of biology: all other conclusions followed from this.

Assimilation, for Hitler, inevitably led to mixed marriages. Such intermixing led to the creation of bastard hybrids, a lowering of the quality of the race as a whole and thus an erosion of its ability to compete in the merciless environment provided by nature. It was no more biologically advisable for a German to mate with a Jew than it was for different species in the animal world to interbreed. It contravened nature's first rule: 'the inner segregation of the species of all living beings on this Earth' (MK, 258). The long-term consequences of this were equally inevitable: 'all great cultures of the past perished only because the originally creative race died out from blood poisoning' (MK, 262).

However, the full significance of the biological language with which Hitler imagined the relationship between Germans and Jews – as separate species whose miscegenation offended the basic principle of nature – can only be understood when we examine more closely the extent to which such biological language was infused with specifically medical imagery and terminology. The phrase 'blood poisoning' was carefully chosen. As the foregoing passage illustrates, Hitler imagined nations themselves as human bodies: as organic creations in which each cell existed not for its own sake but for its essential contribution to the functioning of the whole, and as systems whose organs were under constant attack from parasites, illnesses, poisons or viruses against which they needed constant defence. Such imagery is, again, not accidental, but constantly present in *Mein Kampf.* When describing pre-war Vienna, for example, Hitler tells us that 'if the old hereditary territories were the heart of the Empire, continually driving fresh blood into the circulatory stream of political and cultural life, Vienna was the brain and will in one' (MK, 63).

The national body was, for its part, under constant attack: if the parasite, or 'noxious bacillus' as it is also described here, is not treated in good time and with the requisite thoroughness it will, in time, overcome the 'host' body, which will, in turn, inevitably die. Who played the role of the parasite? The answer, of course, was: the Jews.

Hitler's writings are full of both passing and extended references to Jews which are couched in this medicalized language. Jews are described, variously and repeatedly, as 'the plague of nations', a 'disease', 'tuberculosis', 'parasites', 'poison', a 'foreign virus'. When describing the role of the Jews in Vienna's cultural life he tells us that 'if you cut even cautiously into such an abscess you found, like a maggot in a rotting body, often dazzled by the sudden light – a kike!' (MK, 53). Marxism, we learn, was 'eating like poisonous abscesses into the nation, now here and now there. It seemed as though a continuous stream of poison was being driven into the outermost blood-vessels of this once heroic body . . .' (MK, 141). Sometimes the imagery uses the language of hygiene rather than biology, with the Jews being associated with 'dirt', 'filth' or the absence of cleanliness: the detrimental effect of this on the 'cleanliness' of the national 'body' is equally clear.

What is the significance of this extended medical imagery? To appreciate this fully, we need to return to Hitler's diagnosis (the word is very appropriate) of Germany's defeat in the First World War. For Hitler, the 'body' of the German nation had gone to war to defend itself in the eternal biological struggle for existence, and in pursuit of its essential physical needs. The national body had gone to war fatally weakened, however, by the presence of a poison, bacterium or parasitical illness that was destroying the nation from within and thus undermining its ability to fight. Weakened by this alien parasite, the national body had collapsed and the parasite had emerged triumphant.

If we translate this metaphor back into the human world of politics, its significance becomes chillingly clear. In order to save or to revive the national body, the illness or the parasite has to be eradicated. If it is to go to war once more, the national body must be purged of such harmful influences, restored to full health and able to withstand further attack – otherwise it will only collapse again. Similarly, if we follow through the implications of the language of 'hygiene': the German nation had been infected with dirt, and in order to restore her health the body needed to be cleansed. It is, then, in the medical-biological language through which Hitler depicted Germany's defeat in the First World War that the implicitly genocidal message of *Mein Kampf* is contained. Again, translating the medical language into that of the world of politics: if Germany were to go to war again, she would have to eradicate the malign internal influences that had caused her defeat in the First World War. What were the malign influences? The Marxists who had 'stabbed Germany in the back'. Who were behind the Marxists? The Jews. In other words, regenerating the nation meant eradicating the Jews.

If Hitler's analysis of the nation's problems was expressed in the language of medical diagnosis, moreover, so was his suggestion of a solution. In his *Second Book*, he calls for an 'immunizing defence against every further Jewish danger' (2B, 30); in *Mein Kampf* he tells us that 'poison is countered only by an antidote' (MK, 306). Even more chillingly, he reproduces this idea closely in the *Second Book*, arguing: 'Now, healing the body politic of a profound and serious illness does not involve finding a prescription that is completely free of poison; rather, it is not uncommon to break a poison with a counteracting poison' (2B, 44). Here he acknowledges, effectively, that the 'prescription' (again, the word is not accidental) itself necessitates destroying the offending poison. This particular phrase, it is true, is offered in the context of a discussion of foreign policy, rather than racial policy, but it is so characteristic of Hitler's way of seeing the world that it is difficult not to regard it as highly relevant to his ambitions concerning the Jews.

When we connect these reflections, in turn, to our previous observations concerning the language of 'elimination', 'eradication' and 'extermination' that resonates through Hitler's writing, we have, if not an overt announcement of a genocidal agenda, then at least the rhetorical legitimation of genocide or of a set of ideological positions that contain genocide as a logical possible outcome. It is not possible to see in *Mein Kampf* or the *Second Book* a set of plans or a blueprint for mass murder in any specific way, any more than we can see in the two books a detailed agenda or timetable for foreign policy and war. Such a reading of the texts rests too much on hindsight and an overly literal approach. But, equally, we should not regard Hitler's metaphors merely as metaphors: for him, they described reality.

Certainly the overall message was general enough to indicate the possible existence of numerous different paths that could lead to its implementation, and the process of turning vision into reality inevitably involved considerations that would be worked through according to the needs of the time and context. The creation of that context – the manufacturing of a genocidal climate – created its own challenges too. But the vision of a national body cleansed of its impurities, or cured of its illnesses, was clear, and the implications of this for the Jews of Germany, if not for Europe as a whole, were similarly not hard to deduce. The warning was there for those who wished to heed it.

# 7

# EUGENICS

The racial state must make up for what everyone else today has neglected in this field. It must set race in the centre of all life. It must take care to keep it pure. It must declare the child to be the most precious treasure of the people. It must see to it that only the healthy beget children; but there is only one disgrace: despite one's own sickness and deficiencies, to bring children into the world, and one highest honour: to renounce doing so. And conversely it must be considered reprehensible: to withhold healthy children from the nation. Here the state must act as the guardian of a millennial future in the face of which the wishes and selfishness of the individual must appear as nothing and submit. It must put the most modern medical means in the service of this knowledge. It must declare unfit for propagation all who are in any way visibly sick or who have inherited a disease and can therefore pass it on, and put this into actual practice. Conversely, it must take care that the fertility of the healthy woman is not limited by the financial irresponsibility of a state regime which turns the blessing of children into a curse for the parents. It must put an end to that lazy, nay criminal indifference with which the social premises for a fecund family are treated today, and must instead feel itself to be the highest guardian of this most precious blessing of a people. Its concern belongs more to the child than to the adult.

Those who are physically and mentally unhealthy and unworthy must not perpetuate their suffering in the body of their children. In this the racial state must perform the most gigantic educational task. And some day this will seem to be a greater deed than the most victorious wars of our present bourgeois era. By education it must teach the individual that it is no disgrace, but only a misfortune deserving of pity, to be sick and weakly, but that it is a crime and hence at the same time a disgrace to dishonour one's misfortune by one's own egotism in burdening innocent creatures with it; that by comparison it bespeaks a nobility of highest idealism and the most admirable humanity if the innocently sick, renouncing a child of his own, bestows his love and tenderness upon a poor, unknown young scion of his own nationality, who with his health promises to become some day a powerful member of a powerful community. And in this educational work the state must perform the purely intellectual complement of its practical activity. It must act in this sense without regard to understanding or lack of understanding, approval or disapproval.

A prevention of the faculty and opportunity to procreate on the part of the physically degenerate and mentally sick, over a period of only six hundred years, would not only free humanity from an immeasurable misfortune, but would lead to a recovery which today seems scarcely conceivable. If the fertility of the healthiest bearers of the nationality is

thus consciously and systematically promoted, the result
will be a race which at least will have eliminated the germs
of our present physical and hence spiritual decay.

(MK, 367–8)

So far we have emphasized the presence in Hitler's rhetoric of
many elements of a traditional nineteenth-century nationalist
and racist discourse, whilst recognizing that his ideological
ambitions and his sense of self in relation to the nineteenth-
century past were anything but reactionary. Hitler may have
drawn on a particular canon of nineteenth-century writing for
confirmation of his ideas, he may have reproduced much of
the traditional anti-French rhetoric of nineteenth-century
German nationalism, and much of his anti-Semitic discourse
may have recycled pre-existing stereotypes. But the vision of
regeneration and rebirth that he offered set him apart from the
conservative, dynastic politics of the imperial era, and the
centrality of medical-biological thinking to his anti-Semitic
views marked him out as the representative of a specifically
modern form of racism quite distinct from that which had
prevailed in the nineteenth century.

The explicitly modern dimensions of Hitler's thought are
underlined further when we consider that Hitler's anti-
Semitism did not exist in isolation from other aspects of his
thought but was at the centre of a much broader vision of
social and racial engineering. This vision, which represented
a radicalized form of the eugenicist thinking that was gaining
currency across Europe in the wake of the First World War,
finds its expression in important sections in *Mein Kampf*, of
which the passage above is perhaps the most significant example. It enables us to explore in some detail the nature of
Hitler's illiberalism, the relationship between racist ideology

and totalitarian ambition, and the balance between the conservative and revolutionary aspects of Hitler's rhetoric and belief. It also underlines for us that while the outlines of the 'people's community' are, as previously suggested, often left vague, there is nonetheless in *Mein Kampf* the clear intimation of a legislative programme for central areas of policy for those who wish to recognize it.

As the above passage demonstrates, Hitler rejected the idea that the family and the act of reproduction were matters for private fulfilment only. Such thinking represented for Hitler the outmoded attitudes of the liberal era. The family – and above all the child – were for him the property of the race. The child is not the private property of its parents – it is 'the most precious treasure of the people'. And lest we be inclined to see in this a mere rhetorical flourish, Hitler repeats a few lines later that it is wrong to 'withhold healthy children from the nation': conversely, those who have children to satisfy their own desires but with no regard for the greater needs of the race are guilty of 'egotism'. The message is clear. Those deemed to be healthy have an obligation to produce large families, while those regarded as inferior should not have children at all.

What is also clear, however, is that this is not to be left to the self-policing community. Hitler envisages a central role for the state in the *direction* of reproductive behaviour. It is the state that must make up for previous neglect in this area, it is the state that 'must place race in the centre of all life', and the state that 'must see to it that only the healthy beget children'. The individual's views on this no longer count, for it is the state 'that must act as the guardian of a millennial future in the face of which the wishes and selfishness of the individual must appear as nothing and submit.' Hitler is claiming the absolute right of the state to intervene in the reproductive lives of individuals without the individuals concerned having any form of redress. A more totalitarian ambition than the right to regulate the sexual activity of individuals in this way is hard to imagine.

This passage demonstrates once more the nature of Hitler's totalitarian ambitions: they lie in the claim that the needs of the race have absolute priority over the wishes of the individual, and thus in the conviction that the state has the right to enforce the vital needs of the community over the private wishes of its citizens. The biological metaphors through which Hitler delineated politics are, of course, those that stress that threats to the national body must be eradicated − i.e. resistance must be ruthlessly suppressed − but the suppression of political resistance is a function of something more fundamental: the need for racial regeneration. Hitler's totalitarian aims are certainly not those of one who wishes to wield power for the sake of wielding power alone, but are rooted in a radical vision of social and racial engineering in which the state will be the active agent.

This is not to say that engineering the regenerated race will be pursued through coercion alone. As the above passage shows, Hitler envisaged a key role for propaganda, with the state undertaking 'the most gigantic educational task' in persuading people not to have children if they are deemed to be unhealthy, or encouraging such people to adopt parentless healthy children rather than have children of their own, if the greater needs of the race demand it. There is also the suggestion of practical medical and welfare measures to enable healthy parents to have more children, as in the claim that the state 'must put the most modern medical means in the service of this knowledge', or in his recommendation that financial aid should be given to potential parents who were otherwise forced by the modesty of their monetary circumstances to limit the size of their families.

However, it is equally clear that educational work is not intended to be the limit – only the 'intellectual complement' – of the state's 'practical activity'. For those whom the state wishes to prevent from having children, especially, these passages lay claim to the right to pursue direct intervention in people's bodies in pursuit of the goal. In arguing that the state 'must declare unfit for propagation all who are in any way visibly sick or who have inherited a disease and can therefore pass it on, and put this into actual practice', Hitler is not only underlining his belief in the hereditary nature of illness, he is implying that the state should sterilize those whom it wishes to stop from passing on those illnesses. This may not be spelled out directly, but it is difficult to read this sentence, or the demand that the state 'see to it that only the healthy beget children', in any other way. The insistence, moreover, that the state 'must act in this sense without regard to understanding or lack of understanding, approval or disapproval', contains a clear intimation of exactly how ruthless Hitler intends to be should he ever achieve power. If the 'positive eugenics' or pro-natalist aspects of Hitler's plans confined themselves essentially to the forceful exhortation to the healthy and racially 'fit' to have more children, there is little doubt that the anti-natalist 'negative eugenics' were to involve a far more direct and brutal approach to those whom the state considered unfit to breed.

Can we, then, see in these passages the announcement of an envisaged legislative programme in the field of eugenics? This would perhaps be pushing things too far. However, one cannot read these lines without recalling that in June 1933 the

Law for the Reduction of Unemployment introduced by the new National Socialist regime made provision for marriage loans to be made available to (healthy, 'Aryan' German) married couples in order to encourage women to leave the workplace – with the stipulation that the amount to be repaid would be reduced by one-quarter for each child born to the couple. These measures were followed by the introduction of other financial benefits aimed at alleviating the cost of having children. They were also implemented in a climate in which a general 'cult of motherhood' found expression through numerous symbolic gestures aimed at raising the status of mothers in German society, and in widespread educational initiatives in schools. In other words, both the financial and educational issues addressed by Hitler in the passage discussed here provided the focus of widespread programmes that were embarked upon by the regime from the outset.

Similarly, within six months of establishing itself in power the regime had introduced the Law for the Prevention of Hereditarily Diseased Offspring. Issued in July 1933, this law formalized the right of the state to sterilize forcibly any individual whom its representatives regarded as suffering from a range of (allegedly) hereditary illnesses or from particular physical disabilities. It initiated a massive programme of forced sterilization which led to approximately 350,000 German women and men being rendered infertile against their wishes by 1945.

Both the pro- and anti-natalist ambitions outlined by Hitler in this passage from *Mein Kampf* can, therefore, be directly related to central pieces of the regime's legislative programme implemented from 1933 onwards. On the one hand, the regime introduced a wide range of pro-natalist measures designed to persuade 'suitable' families to have more children;

on the other it embarked upon a brutal programme of forced sterilization as part of an anti-natalist campaign that was far more extreme. Moreover, the balance between exhortation and force exhibited in the pro- and anti-natalist campaigns of the 1930s broadly reflected the balance between exhortation and force intimated in *Mein Kampf*. They remind us again that, while the outlines of the 'people's community' envisaged by Hitler in his writings are in many respects vague and a detailed overall programme is impossible to discern, in specific areas of policy intentions are announced which bear a striking resemblance to measures actually introduced once the regime had come to power. Whilst accepting that we cannot read Hitler's work as a simple statement of intentions whose subsequent implementation we can trace through in a straightforward way, we must also recognize that it is too easy swiftly to dismiss *Mein Kampf* as a guide to his goals.

In other respects, of course, we are left in the dark. In the fields of population and racial policy, this passage in particular offers no forewarning of the evolution of Hitler's agenda for the physically or mentally ill and disabled. The suggestion that the state 'must teach the individual that it is no disgrace, but only a misfortune deserving of pity, to be sick and weakly' contains no hint of the horrors of the 'euthanasia' programme embarked upon by the Nazis when they were in power. This process, which began with the neglect of physically and mentally ill children and adults in the hospitals and asylums of Germany, evolved into the widespread practice of so-called 'mercy killing', and finally became a state-sanctioned policy of mass murder which claimed the lives of at least 70,000 victims. In short, the euthanasia programme, which itself fed into the Holocaust, was hardly driven by the 'pity' mentioned here.

The euthanasia programme provoked some opposition from conservative institutions whose attitudes to the family, to gender roles and to gender relations were superficially similar to Hitler's own. This raises the further question: what was the balance between the conservative and revolutionary aspects of Hitler's thinking on the subject of the family? In some passages of *Mein Kampf* we find a set of attitudes that appear, on the face of it, to echo an essentially conservative vision of the family. In one passage, for example, Hitler argues for the merits of early marriage as a means of combating prostitution and sexually transmitted diseases. Superficially, again, we can see in aspects of Hitler's rhetoric a set of ideas which reproduce a broader traditional or conservative discourse. It is certainly the case that National Socialist propaganda drew much of its force from its ability to address wider pre-existing conservative anxieties about the decline of the nuclear family, the upsetting of gender roles through the upheavals of the First World War, or the blurring of both gender boundaries and sexual norms in the cosmopolitan world of the modern city.

Although there were certainly ideological overlaps between German conservatism and National Socialism in the first half of the century – overlaps which, indeed, grew to the point where the boundaries between the two had in many respects dissolved by the middle of the Second World War – we should remember that many distinctions remained. The more secular aspects of German conservative thinking might have gradually taken on the radicalized trappings of National Socialism, but the overtly Christian dimensions of more mainstream conservative thinking remained distinct, even if, as many scholars have observed, a lot of churchmen were far from immune from the language of anti-Semitism. As the passage above shows, central aspects of National Socialist thinking were simply incompatible with Christian theology or the teachings of the churches, the efforts of 'Nazi theologians' notwithstanding. The suggestion that the regulation of fertility was a matter for the state was anathema to the Christian conviction that conception and birth were God-given gifts; the belief in the inferiority of handicapped or ill children similarly offended Christian notions of the equal sanctity of all human life and the equal value of all humanity before God. The 'pity' described by Hitler was anything but the compassion of the Church.

We noted earlier that the superficial deployment of elements of Christian discourse, such as the language of providence, should not delude us into believing that Hitler's views had any meaningful similarity to those of established religion. More generally, the partial blurring of elements of Hitler's rhetoric with the more traditional elements of nineteenth-century conservatism should not lead us to mistake National Socialism for a reactionary ideological force. As an examination of Hitler's views on eugenics and social engineering makes clear, National Socialism was anything but reactionary. The vision of a racially re-engineered society that Hitler espoused may have been described using language familiar to many on the mainstream right, including, sometimes, the language of an angry Protestant nationalism (this was undoubtedly a key element of the appeal). But the vision itself was far from familiar, and bore no relation to anything recognizable in what earlier nationalist or racist movements had sought to achieve.

The eugenicist vision outlined within this passage encapsulates Hitler's ambition to erect a modern racist state in which the medical and administrative apparatus of government would intervene brutally in the reproductive lives of individuals, in the name of a widespread process of social engineering aimed at regenerating the race. For the racially 'valuable' there was the promise of integration into the 'people's community' as a healthy and productive member of the living national organism. For the 'inferior', there was the prospect of sterilization. For those deemed to be a threat to the community, as we have seen, there was the promise of eradication. We have noted before that few elements of Hitler's thinking can be seen as original, insofar as other expressions of his nationalist, racist and anti-Marxist views can be located in any number of pre-existing texts. Yet moulded together and expressed in such radical and aggressive form, and combined with the broader agenda of eugenic engineering, Hitler's versions cumulatively form a vision of integration and eradication that is qualitatively different. Such a vision finds no counterpart in the nationalist or racist writings of Hitler's predecessors and, despite the traditional trappings of some of his rhetoric, it marks out the essentially modern quality of Hitler's thought.

# 8

## MODERNITY

The issue of eugenics and the suggestion that Hitler's vision of a racially engineered new society marked him out from the old-style conservative nationalists of the previous century, raise a broader contentious issue – that of Hitler's attitude towards modernity as a whole. Traditionally, Hitler's has been seen as a determinedly atavistic ideology, with his admiration of healthy peasant life and his dislike of urban culture reflecting a desire to 're-agrarianize' Germany, to turn back the clock and put the industrial revolution into reverse, recreating Germany as a pre-industrial idyll. The very traditional images of peasants created by later National Socialist propaganda certainly imply that an element of ruralist romanticism informed the regime's views. However, Hitler has relatively little to say about peasants or rural life in his main writings, so the suggestion that he intended to 're-agrarianize' Germany can by no means be accepted as obvious or incontrovertible. Furthermore, the ideas discussed in the preceding chapter, linked as they were with concepts being developed in some of the most respected modern scientific and medical institutions of the time, and with their own pseudo-scientific claims to

rationality hardly suggest that Hitler was a determined opponent of the modern world in all its aspects.

There is, though, certainly much in his writings to sustain
the idea that he hated Germany's cities in their modern form.
Consider, for example, this passage from the *Second Book*:

> [A] particular danger of the so-called peaceful economic
> policy of a people lies in the fact that it initially enables an
> increase in the population that in the end will no longer be
> in any proportion to the productivity of the people's own
> land and territory. Not infrequently, this crowding of too
> many people into an inadequate living space also leads to
> difficult social problems, as people are now gathered into
> work centres that do not resemble cultural centres so much
> as abscesses on the body of the people in which all evils,
> vices and sicknesses seem to unite. They are above all
> hotbeds of blood-mixing and bastardization, and thus
> mostly also of race degeneration, thus resulting in those
> purulent herds in which the maggots of the international
> Jewish community thrive and cause the ultimate decay of
> the people.
>
> (2B, 27)

Many of the aspects of Hitler's thought that we have discussed
at various previous points collide in this extract; it is one of a
number of passages in which he criticizes the modern city.
Most obviously, the links between the peaceful economic
policy that he rejected, the decline in the race's ability to feed
itself, the resort to 'internal colonization' and urbanization
and thus the weakening of the race through 'blood-mixing'
and contact with the Jews underline in telling fashion the
connections that Hitler drew between commercialism and

racial decline. But what is also striking is Hitler's proclivity, particularly pronounced here, to switch constantly between different modes of description, sometimes, indeed, within single sentences. He starts one sentence with reference to 'living space' and 'work centres' and finishes it by talking about 'abscesses' in the national 'body' and 'sicknesses'; he begins the next by talking about 'bastardization', slipping in turn effortlessly back into discussion of 'purulent herds' and Jewish 'maggots'. This constant shift into and out of biological and medical metaphors warns us again that we should not see in them mere images that Hitler distinguished from the real world he felt he was describing.

If the rural world is not explicitly described in this passage, then the contrast is implicit enough. If the city is a centre of 'evil, vice and sickness', and a site of 'blood mixing and bastardization', then its rural counterpart, we may safely assume, stands for everything clean, healthy and wholesome, and is the guarantor of racial purity. It is something to be cherished and preserved. (In the few passages in which the peasantry is discussed in *Mein Kampf* we find this confirmed.) The little that Hitler does say is quite clear: 'the possibility of preserving a healthy peasant class as a foundation for a whole nation can never be valued highly enough. Many of our present-day sufferings are only the consequence of the unhealthy relationship between rural and city population' (MK, 126). Elsewhere, moreover, we find straightforward critiques of the ongoing process of migration from countryside to city which was taking place in Germany at that time. Hitler contrasts the man who makes 'an honest living from the peasant sod' (MK, 24) with the man who migrates to the city and lives in surroundings that 'poison his soul' (MK, 25). The imagery is very similar to that in the first passage quoted in this chapter: cities are unclean places in every sense of the word, places in which the healthy become poisoned. The motif works here, as elsewhere, on two levels: the newly arrived peasant-turned-worker is poisoned politically by his contact with Marxism, pacifism and democracy, and he – and by extension the nation as a whole – is also poisoned physically by sexual contact with Jews, prostitutes or foreigners. The poisoning of the body translates into an erosion of national reliability. Describing migrant workers in pre-war Vienna Hitler tells us: 'When they arrived, they belonged to their people; after remaining for a few years, they were lost to it' (MK, 25).

Not only does Hitler argue the merits of the rural over the urban, however: implicit in much of his discussion about the need for living space, and indeed explicitly stated in the occasional passing sentence, is a strong sense that expansion into new living space is to be driven by the settlement of peasants. The repeated use of the image of 'the sword and the plough' as the twin guarantors of Germany's continued existence and prosperity certainly suggests that the glorious new Empire is to be based on agriculture, not industry. Elsewhere, Hitler is more explicit, informing the reader that: 'there are at the present time immense areas of unused soil, only waiting for the men to till them' (MK, 123). While the 'racial commissions' that Hitler advocates to select the most racially valuable members of the nation for settlement in 'border colonies' are not specifically charged with the task of selecting peasants as the bearers of the new imperial mission, it is fair to assume that this was what he had in mind.

None of this, however, adds up to an argument that Hitler actually wished to 're-agrarianize' Germany. Hitler speaks of the need to preserve the peasantry, and of the peasantry as the foundation of a healthy nation. He also clearly wishes to overcome the negative effects of urbanization. The colonial mission is also to be pursued in the form of agricultural settlement. But nowhere does Hitler speak of reversing industrialization or urbanization as such, and it is hard to believe that he imagined this as a feasible project for Germany. Indeed, other passages in his writing suggest an admiration for industrial modernity which is very difficult to square with the vision of wholesale re-agrarianization that some detect in his work. Consider, for example, this description of the United States of America, found in his *Second Book*:

> The size and the wealth of its internal market permit production levels and thus production facilities that decrease the cost of the product to such a degree that, despite the enormous wages, underselling no longer seems at all possible. The development of the automotive industry can serve as a cautionary example here. It is not only that we Germans, for example, despite our laughable wages, are not in a position to export successfully against American competition even to a small degree, but that we must also look on as American cars are proliferating even in our own country. This is only possible because the size of the internal American market and its wealth of buying power and also, again, raw materials guarantee the American automobile industry internal sales figures that alone permit production methods which would simply be impossible in Europe due to the lack of internal sales opportunities. The result of that is the enormous export capacity of the American automobile industry. At issue is the general motorization of the world – a matter of immeasurable future significance. For the replacement of human and animal power by the engine is only at the beginning of

its development; the end cannot yet be assessed at all
today. For the American Union, in any case, today's auto-
mobile industry is at the forefront of all other industries.

(2B, 107)

The utopian vision of the future encapsulated in the new
Fordist model of industrial and social modernization was
regarded by Europeans with a mixture of admiration, fascination and horror. While European industry continued to
produce low quantities of high-quality goods using methods
that relied heavily on highly skilled labour, and thus suffered
from high labour costs per unit produced, American industry
had revolutionized – or at least begun to revolutionize – its
production methods. The new mass production pioneered by
Henry Ford, with its emphasis on division of labour, repeti-
tion of task, coordinated production flows and assembly-line
routine represented simultaneously an inspiration and a threat
to Europeans of all political persuasions. The lowering of unit
costs meant that goods could be produced and sold much
more cheaply; increased efficiency meant that, despite widespread deskilling, workers could be paid higher wages. Lower
prices and higher wages provided the key to creating a consumer idyll in which the interests of the workers and those of
the owners would meet.

At the time when Hitler wrote the preceding passage the
United States was at the absolute height of the consumer
boom of the 1920s, and it is not difficult to detect in his
words a degree of admiration for the widespread mechaniza-
tion of production and the motorization of American society.
Much as he disliked the effects of the industrial revolution on
Germany, there was much in the Fordist model that appealed
to Hitler. Firstly, Ford's message was an avowedly populist

one: cars were not just for the rich, they were for all. This chimed with the egalitarianism in Hitler's vision of the 'people's community' — with the idea that all politically and racially acceptable Germans should have access to goods hitherto reserved for the elites, whom Hitler derided as the 'upper ten thousand'. Second, there were clear similarities between the vision of class harmony present in the Fordist dream and that embodied in the 'people's community' that Hitler sought to create — as we have already seen, Hitler wished to abolish the 'cleavage' between the classes.

Hitler's fascination with the alternative model of modernity that was apparently being created before his eyes in the United States deserves our attention, not only because it suggests a very different side to Hitler's world-view from that with which most people are familiar but because certain projects and policies pursued by the National Socialist regime during the 1930s bear more than a passing resemblance to the utopian mass society represented in the Fordist vision. Not only did Hitler pursue the 'motorization' of German society in the 1930s, introducing measures to stimulate the car industry and initiating the *Autobahn* project, he also specifically modelled the plans for the new 'Volkswagen' or 'People's Car' on Ford's River Rouge plant. Such mass production was not just confined to cars: the 1930s witnessed a significant expansion in Germany's production and ownership of radios — the obvious aim of which, of course, was to extend the reach of the regime's propaganda. More generally, housing projects, factory health and hygiene regimes, and company sports and social activities introduced in Germany in the 1930s have more than an echo of the rationalized society envisioned by Ford and others and described in the passage concerned.

How much, though, should we read into this? What is the relative importance of the genocidal message and the fascination with motor cars in Hitler's writings? It is instructive to note that during the 1930s and early 1940s the genocidal project was pursued to its terrifying climax, while only a handful of Volkswagen cars were ever produced under the Nazis. As far as the writings themselves are concerned, the implicitly genocidal message of *Mein Kampf* is deeply embedded in the entire text, while Hitler's expressed thoughts on the United States consist essentially of a few passages in the *Second Book*. Moreover, we gain a distorted image of Hitler's view of the United States if we confine ourselves to a reading of the sections in which he discusses the implications of Fordism:

> It is not by chance that the American union is the state in which by far the greatest number of bold, sometimes unbelievably so, inventions are currently taking place. Compared to old Europe, which has lost an infinite amount of its best blood through war and emigration, the American nation appears as a young, racially select people [. . .] Only a deliberately racial policy could save the European nations from losing the power of the initiative to America as a result of the lower value of the European peoples in comparison to the Americans. But when instead the German people allows – in addition to a Jewish-instigated systematic bastardization with inferior human material, and a resulting decline of its racial value itself – the best blood-lines to be removed through the ongoing emigration of hundreds upon hundreds of thousands of individual specimens, it will gradually deteriorate into an inferior and therefore incapable and worthless people. The danger is

particularly great since – with complete indifference on our part – the American union itself, motivated by the teachings of its own racial researchers, established specific standards for immigration. By making an immigrant's ability to set foot on American soil dependent on specific racial requirements on the one hand as well as a certain level of physical health of the individual himself the bleeding Europe of its best people has effectively become regulated and bound by law [. . .]

(2B, 109–110)

This passage underlines once more how Hitler explained all human affairs in terms of race and racial struggle, and suggests the need for great caution when arguing that his understanding of the United States provided the basis for pursuing the creation of a classically modern economy and society in Germany. Hitler did not explain American economic success in terms of economics. He saw in it merely further confirmation of his theories that emigration from Europe had led to a fall in the racial value of its remaining citizens, and thus to the inevitable decline in her competitive position vis-à-vis the new power of the United States. While the United States progressed, Germany continued to suffer from the malign influence of the Jews. The solution was not, therefore, to import American production methods or to pursue the economic policies of the United States: it was to implement the racial policy that he demanded. The fact that the United States government had recently introduced two important pieces of immigration legislation – the 'special standards for immigration' of which Hitler speaks are a reference to the Immigration Acts of 1921 and 1924 – was simply further proof of this. The possibility that the United States, as the

modern land of immigration par excellence, owed its economic and cultural vibrancy precisely to its ethnic diversity
and to its celebration of the 'melting pot' was not something
that Hitler chose to consider. The greatest irony of all, of
course, was that a very significant proportion of the American
immigrants in the decades prior to the 1920s had been those
very East Europeans whom Hitler regarded with such disdain;
and a significant proportion of these had been Jewish.

Ultimately, then, it is difficult to see in Hitler's discussions
of the United States in the *Second Book* anything that would
lead us seriously to believe that Hitler had an informed, well-
considered vision of the transformation of Germany into a
modern, upwardly mobile, consumerist industrial society.
Rather, his insistence on explaining contemporary American
economic developments in terms of the usual overarching
racial theories, and his hopelessly inaccurate understanding of
American immigration history underline something else: his
woeful ignorance of matters outside his own immediate experience, and the poverty of thought in his work as a whole.

Where, then, does consideration of these passages leave
our understanding of Hitler's vision of modernity? The message is, perhaps, ambiguous. On the one hand, Hitler clearly
venerated the imagined superiority of rural life, and saw in the
supposedly healthy peasantry the source of the regeneration of
the race; it was the peasantry who would till the newly
acquired lands conquered by the resurgent nation and who
would thus provide the people with their essential needs. The
cities, by contrast, were seen as dens of vice, sedition and
racial decay: purifying the national body would mean cleansing it of the malign political and biological influences that the
city both represented and contained. However, at least some
passages in Hitler's writing suggest a slightly more positive

attitude to some features of industrial modernity. While these hardly give grounds for believing that Hitler wished to foster the transition to an Americanized form of modernity – a form about which he was in any case ill-informed – they do suggest that we ought to exercise caution before reading into his writings a one-sided advocacy of re-agrarianization. There is, indeed, little in either *Mein Kampf* or the *Second Book* to suggest that he envisaged this.

We should not shy away, ultimately, from concluding that Hitler's ideas in this area are contradictory, incomplete, or just lacking in focus. At best, we might suggest that his books imply a vision – one that was struggling to get out – of an alternative modernity that would maintain a harmonious balance between town and country. It would be based on the values and practices of rural society but would include healthy cities in which workers, rescued from the pernicious influences of Marxism and reconciled to the nation, would take their full place in a *Volksgemeinschaft* in which tensions between peasants' interests and those of industrial workers would have been gloriously overcome – instead of working just for themselves, all would now work for the nation.

## 9

# EXPANSION

We National Socialists must never under any circumstances join in the foul hurrah-patriotism of our present
bourgeois world. In particular it is mortally dangerous to
regard the last pre-War developments as binding even in
the slightest degree for our own course. From the whole
historical development of the nineteenth century, not a
single obligation can be derived which was grounded
in this period itself. In contrast to the conduct of the
representatives of this period, we must again profess the
highest aim of all foreign policy, to wit: to bring the soil
into harmony with the population. Yes, from the past we
can only learn that, in setting an objective for our political
activity, we must proceed in two directions: land and soil
as the goal of our foreign policy, and a new philosophically
established, uniform foundation as the aim of political
activity at home.

(MK, 593)

The internal goals of creating a 'people's community' and
embarking upon racial regeneration were not, of course, ends

in themselves. Nor could they be, according to Hitler's view of history: a newly resurgent nation would inevitably have to seek living space abroad. Sometimes in his writings, as in this passage, it appears that domestic renewal and external expansion are to go hand in hand; in other passages, he implies that the one is the precondition for the other. Elsewhere in *Mein Kampf*, he argues, for example, that 'only the elimination of the causes of our collapse, as well as the destruction of its beneficiaries, can create the premise for our outward fight for freedom' (MK, 555). Either way, the two aims were clearly inextricably linked in Hitler's mind.

The task of any nation's foreign policy was to match the nation's living space to the size and needs of its population. As we have seen, Hitler rejected the idea that the growth of the population could be artificially limited; he also rejected the possibility of 'internal colonization'. The only possible foreign-policy options were either a peaceful, trade-based campaign of overseas colonialism, or territorial expansion through military means. As we have also seen, Hitler constantly and repeatedly rejected the idea that *Weltpolitik* provided any form of model. The preceding passage offers a further clear expression of this. But, beyond this, the passage is significant for its absolute disavowal of the suggestion that the foreign policy of the nineteenth century offered any positive starting points for contemporary policy. For sure, this radical position served Hitler's political needs at the time of writing. The sarcastic dismissal of the 'foul hurrah-patriotism of our present bourgeois world' is one of many references to his competitors on the nationalist wing of German politics with which he makes clear his disdain for the old-style politics of the right. Indeed, the texts of *Mein Kampf* and the *Second Book* are littered with dismissive digs at 'beer-table patriotism' (2B, 62), 'inflated parlour patriots' (MK, 579), or 'petit bourgeois café politicians' (MK, 579). The consistency with which Hitler resorted to such sideswipes reminds us that in his writing in the 1920s he was constantly seeking to establish forcefully his status as the most radical representative of the nationalist movement.

This was not merely short-term political expediency, however: it reflected Hitler's basic beliefs. To begin with, he rejected vigorously the suggestion that the foreign-policy aims of the new Germany could ever be restricted to a return to the borders of 1914, describing this as a 'political absurdity' (MK, 593). In other words, the reversal of the punitive restrictions of the Treaty of Versailles was not to be an end in itself but at best a means to an end. Beyond this, however, Hitler was critical of the entire alliance policy of the pre-1914 era. Castigating the 'aimlessness and incompetence' (MK, 590) of previous foreign policy, and scorning the 'political incapacity of the [. . .] bunglers of the mishandled Reich' (2B, 64*), he reserved some of his strongest and most trenchant criticisms for the pre-war policy of maintaining an alliance with Austria-Hungary. This alliance, he argued, had been pursued for dynastic purposes rather than to serve the needs of the people. Not only had it forced Germany to refrain from any further attempt to unite the Germans of Austria with the Reich; it had been compelled by diplomatic niceties to remain passively on the sidelines as the multinational, multi-ethnic Austro-Hungarian Empire had pursued policies that reduced the status and power of the traditionally dominant German element.

* I have used the 1961 translation here; the page reference refers to that edition.

The result had been a foreign policy that ran counter to all the fundamental interests of the German race, and which had led the nation into a war she could not win. Pursuit of a trade-based foreign policy, rather than one based on racial considerations, had led to conflict with Britain; misguided friendship with Austria-Hungary had led inevitably to conflict with Russia. Germany had thus found herself encircled and tied to the fortunes of a fading star condemned by its ethnic diversity to accelerated decline. The outcome of the war was thus inevitable, especially given Germany's internal weaknesses. Instead, Hitler demanded a land-based policy of expansion into areas adjacent to the mother country: 'The point of a healthy territorial policy lies in the expansion of a people's living space by allocating to the excess population new areas for colonization; however, if this process is not to take on the character of emigration, the colony must maintain close political and national relations with the mother country' (2B, 77).

Where, however, was this to be? How far was it to extend? Did Hitler envisage endless expansion? Endless expansion is perhaps implicit in Hitler's belief in the permanence of the racial struggle and the correspondingly temporary nature of any political borders. But Hitler's foreign policy, like any other, had to be implemented in a specific time and place, within a particular political context and despite numerous constraints. Our analysis of *Mein Kampf* and the *Second Book* is thus incomplete if we content ourselves with the uncontroversial assertion that Hitler envisaged war and expansion at some point. We need to ask whether a concrete programme of any kind is discernible, and where, precisely, such expansion was to occur.

Some of the most convoluted passages of *Mein Kampf* are those in which Hitler outlines his foreign-policy ambitions, and the precise parameters of those ambitions are not always easy to detect. Again, the interpretative challenge lies in accepting that much of the vision espoused is quite general and based on arguments that are not entirely free of contradiction, whilst being careful not to miss the messages that are clearly there. When Hitler steps back from the what-ifs and what-might-have-beens of Germany's historic alliance policies and offers more general reflections on the future goals of the nation, one can see the outlines of a foreign-policy agenda recognizably related to the 1930s and 1940s.

The cornerstone of Hitler's future ambitions was clearly an alliance with Britain. This should be pursued despite the recent experience of the First World War, for 'an alliance policy is not conducted from the standpoint of retrospective grudges, but is fructified by the knowledge of retrospective experience' (MK, 564). Such experience should teach Germany the folly of fighting a war with the British Empire, so Hitler argued; for Britain's part, Germany's collapse and current weak state meant that British policy would no longer be geared to preventing German hegemony on the Continent. Quite the opposite: since 1918, the new threat to Britain was France. As a consequence, 'England's policy from year to year must be directed more and more to an obstruction of France's unlimited drive for hegemony' (MK, 564).

For Germany's part, 'the inexorable mortal enemy of the German people is and remains France' (MK, 565). Britain might oppose Germany's resurrection; France opposed her very existence. As long as Germany refrained from the misguided colonial policy that had brought her into conflict with Britain before, there was sufficient common interest in pursuing an anti-French policy for a closer relationship to emerge.

Much of the foreign-policy rhetoric of *Mein Kampf* and the *Second Book* is, indeed, directed against France. In part, as we have seen, this represents a continuation of very traditional forms of German nationalist rhetoric; in part, too, it reflected Hitler's own war experience, which was spent entirely on the Western Front. The conventional nationalist revisionism of the immediate post-war years also focused its anger strongly on France. Despite Hitler's efforts to distance himself from the broader nationalist movement, and although he had certainly moved beyond this position by the time he wrote *Mein Kampf*, we can still see many echoes of this stance in Hitler's writing. More recently, of course, France had provoked the renewed hostility of German nationalism through her occupation of the Ruhr in 1923, which also accounts for some of the radical anti-French tone of *Mein Kampf*. Above all, acting through France, it seems, were now even darker forces: 'The armies of France must, therefore, besiege the German state structure until the Reich, inwardly exhausted, succumbs to the Bolshevistic shock troop of international Jewish world finance' (MK, 568).

However, it would be wrong to conclude from this anti-French language that the living space which Hitler intended to acquire for Germany was to be found in the west. The key foreign-policy passage in *Mein Kampf* is probably the following one:

And so we National Socialists consciously draw a line beneath the foreign policy tendency of our pre War period. We take up where we broke off six hundred years ago. We stop the endless German movement to the south and west, and turn our gaze towards the land in the east. At long last we break off the colonial and commercial policy of the pre-War period and shift to the soil policy of the future.

If we speak of soil in Europe today, we can primarily have in mind only Russia and her vassal border states.

(MK, 598)

For Hitler, then, living space was to be found in the east. During the nineteenth century, he believed, cooperation with Russia had been a theoretical possibility. Had Germany wished to pursue her policy of conflict with Britain, then she should have done so after having secured an alliance with Russia – this would certainly have been preferable to the policy of alliance with Austria-Hungary. Now, however, such an alliance was completely out of the question. Since 1917, Russia had been dominated by the Bolsheviks – behind whom, of course, stood the Jews. Conquering living space thus also depended upon defeating Germany's mortal enemy. By the mid-1920s, the firm link in Hitler's mind between Marxism and the international Jewish conspiracy was such that for him political, military and ideological factors all pointed in one direction: towards an attack on the Soviet Union.

In answer to those on the nationalist right who continued to argue that German revival could be pursued in alliance with the Soviet Union, Hitler resorted to his favourite biological metaphors: 'If a man believes that he can enter into profitable connections with parasites, he is like a tree trying to conclude for its own profit an agreement with a mistletoe' (MK, 604). The interchangeability of political and biological terms is again telling. To unite Germany, Hitler had to defeat the Marxists. To restore the health of the national body, he had to eradicate the poison. To feed the people, he had to acquire living space in the east. To save Germany from destruction, he had to defeat the Jewish-Bolshevik state. The different modes of description were indistinguishable in Hitler's mind. Either way, 'The fight against Jewish world Bolshevization requires a clear attitude towards Soviet Russia. You cannot drive out the Devil with Beelzebub' (MK, 605).

Interesting again in the preceding passage is the sense that in turning towards the east Germany will be connecting with the positive traditions of a deep mythical past: in this case, in taking up 'where we broke off six hundred years ago' Hitler will be reviving the activities of the medieval Teutonic knights. Yet again, the tradition within which Hitler saw himself standing was not that of Bismarck, nor of the Kaiser, but was part of a far longer continuum, one that he regarded the policies of recent decades as having broken. National rebirth was not seen by Hitler in terms of restoring the pre-1914 situation: the 1914 borders were themselves the product of a wrong-headed policy. The specifically fascist element in Hitler's radical nationalism is again revealed in his contrast of a recent past marked by decay and error with the presence of positive historical traditions that lay buried in the deeper past but were ready to be reborn.

Not only did Hitler envisage expansion in a different direction, he also had a quite different image of the nature of colonial rule:

> The racial state [. . .] could under absolutely no circumstances annex Poles with the intention of turning them into Germans one day. On the contrary, it would have to decide either to seal off these alien racial elements in order to prevent the repeated contamination of one's own people's blood, or it would have to remove them entirely, transferring the land and territory that thus became free to its own national comrades.
>
> (2B, 53)

> The movement will never see subjugated, so-called Germanized Czechs or Poles as a strengthening of the

nation or of the people, rather this represents a racial weakening of our people. For its national conception is not
determined by earlier patriotic conceptions of the state, but
rather by ethnic, racial insights.

(2B, 49)

By the 'vassal border states' of Russia, then, Hitler primarily
meant Poland and Czechoslovakia. But the form of domination he envisaged was, as these short passages show, not that
of the Austro-Hungarian Empire, nor indeed of the former
German Reich. Hitler did not believe in the possibility of a
viable multi-ethnic empire – this had been the lesson of
his years in Vienna – and he did not believe that members
of other ethnic groups could be turned into reliable sub-
jects. This ran counter to the basic laws of nature and
human history. Neither did he believe in the possibility of
'Germanization' through the suppression of subject peoples'
languages or religious life, as had occurred in areas of mixed
German-Polish settlement during the pre-1914 imperial era.
These missed the point, just as the idea that Jews could assim-
ilate as Germans missed the point, which was that fundamental
issues of racial purity were at stake.

Instead, as these passages show, Hitler insisted that Poles
should be 'sealed off' or 'removed'. It would have been no
more possible to forecast accurately from these short sentences the widespread practices of ghettoization, expulsion
and 'resettlement' that occurred in such murderous fashion
in the occupied east between 1939 and 1945 than it would
have been to predict with absolute certainty that Auschwitz
would be the necessary culmination of the translation of
'biological' anti-Semitic ideology into action after 1933. But
the passages do contain a clear intimation of a system of

colonial domination quite unlike that experienced by Poles under the German Emperor or by the subject nationalities of the Austro-Hungarian Empire before 1918. They do, moreover, *imply* ghettoization, expulsion and 'resettlement' as logical possible outcomes; given what we can discern from *Mein Kampf* as a whole about Hitler's genocidal mentality, the likelihood that these *possible* outcomes, or something like them, would have been the *actual* outcomes may be regarded as a strong one.

Thus far, we have suggested that the focus of Hitler's pursuit of living space was Russia and have noted from short passing remarks that the vision of colonial domination he espoused was a very harsh one that fitted with the general pattern of his racist ways of thinking. But can we go further, and see in his writings a more specific and detailed foreign-policy programme? Here, the answer is undoubtedly 'no'. Any 'programme' must be discerned through logical deduction rather than through exegesis of the texts themselves. Hitler intended to reverse the Treaty of Versailles, to reunite all ethnic Germans within one 'national community', to defeat the 'vassal border states' of Russia and to attack Russia herself. For conventional great-power and strategic reasons he also intended to defeat France. He aimed to achieve all this through alliance with Great Britain and (further analysis would show) with Italy too. That much is clear from a mixture of extended passages and passing references, as well as inference from Hitler's rhetoric. Whether Hitler imagined a process of permanent expansion going beyond the defeat of the Soviet Union is impossible to say from a reading simply of what *Mein Kampf* and the *Second Book* have to say about foreign policy but Hitler's view of history points that way.

But while political, military and simple geographical logic dictated a broad sequence of events to be followed – it was impossible to attack the Soviet Union before Germany had rearmed, most obviously – this vision could still be pursued in a number of different ways. As such, it remained vague and general. Nor does Hitler anywhere in his two books offer anything remotely recognizable as a timetable for action. Most references to the future in his writings of the 1920s suggest timescales for national regeneration stretching forward over many generations. Whether it may be safely assumed that Hitler imagined a similar timescale for colonial expansion is open to question – this would certainly sit uneasily with his growing sense of himself as a man of destiny chosen by fate to lead the German people to renewed strength. But the lack of clarity in this respect underlines the fact that Hitler's vision of a new German empire stretching into the east was precisely that – a vision – and that Hitler himself was not a planner or a formulator of detailed programmes. His politics were entirely of the visionary kind.

# 10

# LEADERSHIP, PROPAGANDA, MOBILIZATION

We have already seen that *Mein Kampf* is to be read, in part, as a document of the leadership struggles affecting the German far right in the 1920s, and in part as a statement of Hitler's emerging belief in himself as a man destined to lead the revitalization of the German nation. Beyond this, however, the text contains much of value to those seeking to understand his beliefs on political leadership, his attitudes to democracy, his views on the relationship between successful political movements and the masses, and – to a much lesser extent – his conception of the coming National Socialist state.

> Any man who wants to be leader bears, along with the highest unlimited authority, also the ultimate and heaviest responsibility.
>
> Anyone who is not equal to this or is too cowardly to bear the consequences of his acts is not fit to be leader; only the hero is cut out for this.
>
> The progress and culture of humanity are not a product of the majority, but rest exclusively on the genius and energy of the personality.

> To cultivate the personality and establish it in its rights is one of the prerequisites for recovering the greatness and power of our nationality.
>
> Hence the movement is anti-parliamentarian, and even its participation in a parliamentary institution can only imply activity for its destruction, for eliminating an institution in which we must see one of the gravest symptoms of mankind's decay.
>
> (MK, 313)

Hitler rejected the Weimar Republic because he associated it with the malign forces of the Jewish-inspired revolution of November 1918, and because he blamed it for having accepted the armistice and the hated Treaty of Versailles. He also attributed to it – quite unfairly – the responsibility for the chaotic, inflation-ridden state of post-war Germany. However, this hatred of the Republic was not only rooted in hatred of the particular brand of Weimar democracy. Hitler rejected democracy in principle.

To Hitler, democracy inevitably led to the rule of the inferior: 'sooner will a camel pass through a needle's eye than a great man be "discovered" by an election' (MK, 81). Natural leaders – so-called 'personalities' – were always marginalized by a system that fostered a levelling-down of all political talents. That system attracted into parliament mediocre figures whose sole interest lay in adapting their policies to the constantly changing whims of the masses, in order that they might retain their parliamentary majorities and thus continue to enjoy the trappings of power. Parliamentarians were at best 'mentally dependent nonentities' (MK, 83), at worst they were 'gangsters'. Worst of all, as far as the system itself was concerned, the transient nature of parliamentary majorities meant that no one could ever be held fully responsible for wrong decisions. All that happened was that a government which had taken wrong decisions, however catastrophic, would be forced to resign. A new government would be created, one that was not fundamentally different to its predecessor, and the people were forced to bear the consequences.

Created as they were through a system whereby each member of the community, whether strong or weak, enjoyed equal influence – through their individual vote – and resting on a process of debate and consensus-seeking rather than hard conflict, parliamentary structures offended the 'aristocratic principle of Nature': the notion that life was a struggle between unequal people and that the strong had no obligations whatsoever to the weak. It came as no surprise, then, to learn that the principle of equality upon which democracy was based was an invention of the Jews. In both *Mein Kampf* and the *Second Book* Jews are referred to as 'wirepullers' – the clear implication being that democracy had been foisted on the German people by an alien conspiracy intent upon accelerating the nation's decline.

In place of this Hitler advocated the 'leadership principle'. Drawing on the model provided, so he felt, by the imperial German army, he demanded that discussion should be replaced by obedience, and that authority from the bottom up – the democratic principle – should be replaced by authority from the top down. Those in power had to enjoy 'unlimited authority', as this passage suggests, but they alone shouldered the responsibility for their decisions and they alone would be called to account if they erred.

What – according to Hitler – constituted a good leader? He had to be, firstly, someone in command of the correct theoretical insights – by which, of course, Hitler meant an appreciation of the laws of history as racial struggle and the need to judge all political questions on grounds of racial necessity. This, however, was not enough. The experience of the pre-war Viennese Pan Germans, under Georg von Schoenerer, whom Hitler admired in many ways, showed that having the right ideas was insufficient. The leader must also be a good organizer. Because the ability to organize people depended on being able to understand them, the leader must also be a psychologist: 'an agitator who demonstrates the ability to transmit an idea to the broad masses must always be a psychologist, even if he were only a demagogue' (MK, 528). Being just one, or even two of these things was not enough: a great leader had to be all of them. Theory was no use if one could not galvanize people into following its insights. Conversely, there was no point in being able to mobilize a large following if one did not have the correct understanding of why one was doing this. For this reason, great leaders seldom announced themselves: 'the combination of theoretician, organizer and leader in one person is the rarest thing that can be found on this Earth; this combination makes the great man' (MK, 528).

Above all, according to Hitler, 'leading means: being able to move masses' (MK, 528). Central to this was, of course, propaganda:

> The art of propaganda lies in understanding the emotional ideas of the great masses and finding, through a psycho-logically correct form, the way to the attention and thence to the heart of the broad masses. The fact that our bright boys do not understand this merely shows how mentally lazy and conceited they are.
>
> Once we understand how necessary it is for propaganda to be adjusted to the broad mass, the following rule results:

It is a mistake to make propaganda many-sided, like scientific instruction, for instance.

The receptivity of the great mass is very limited, their intelligence is small, but their power of forgetting is enormous. In consequence of these facts, all effective propaganda must be limited to a very few points and must harp on these in slogans until the last member of the public understands what you want him to understand by your slogan. As soon as you sacrifice this slogan and try to be many-sided, the effect will piddle away, for the crowd can neither digest nor retain the material offered. In this way the result is weakened and in the end entirely cancelled out.

(MK, 165)

Hitler's belief in the importance of correct propaganda was, like so many things, a product of his analysis of Germany's failings during the First World War. Germany had lost partly because of her failure to mobilize the masses behind the war. This was because her propaganda had been inferior to that of the British, who, unlike the Germans, had successfully communicated to the people the importance of the fight: 'all our studying had to be done on the enemy side, for the activity on our side was modest, to say the least' (MK, 161). His assessment of the propaganda achievements of Germany during the First World War was damning. He maintained that 'the total miscarriage of the German "enlightenment" service stared every soldier in the face . . .' (MK, 161). Not only had propaganda for the soldiers been inadequate, it had also been found wanting on the home front. In Germany, an inability to define war aims that spoke to the needs of the people, rather than to those of big business or the governing dynasty, and a failure to convey to the masses the significance of this life-and-death struggle for the race as a whole meant that the government had not integrated the workers behind the war effort. This failure, in turn, had helped to pave the way for the November 1918 revolution.

For all his populist rhetoric, Hitler had a low opinion of the ability of the masses to absorb complex messages. As this passage shows, he believed that propaganda should be kept simple, that it should appeal to the emotions, or to 'the heart', rather than to reason. Times of war were not moments to engage in sweet reasoning: they were periods of struggle to the death, and it could not be the task of propaganda to recognize the reasonable claims of others and weigh them against one's own. To do this was to invite doubt among the masses as to the rightness of the nation's cause, and thus to allow weakness to set in. Rather, war propaganda should insist one-sidedly on the absolute rightness of one's own cause, irrespective of the merits of the case.

Propaganda did not only exist to serve the nation in times of war. It also had a crucial role to play in political mobilization. Hitler had a shrewd understanding of the importance of the crowd in political propaganda. It is in the mass meeting that a new supporter, who may, in joining the movement, have gone out on a limb from his friends or colleagues, 'for the first time gets the picture of a larger community, which in most people has a strengthening, encouraging effect' (MK, 435). Hitler argued that when a new supporter 'steps for the first time into a mass meeting and has thousands and thousands of people of the same opinion around him, when, as a seeker, he is swept away by three or four thousand others into the mighty effect of suggestive intoxication and enthusiasm, when the visible success and agreement of thousands confirm to him the rightness of the new doctrine and for the first time arouse doubt in the truth of his previous conviction – then he himself has succumbed to the magic influence of what we designate as "mass suggestion"' (MK, 435).

It is worth dwelling on this sentence, for its implications run counter to what is often understood by the term 'propaganda' and its role in generating support for the National Socialist movement. Propaganda does not function through 'brainwashing' – this is far too crude an understanding of how even the most tyrannical totalitarian regime functions. For Hitler, propaganda was clearly not intended to dupe people into believing something that they did not already believe. Although, as this sentence suggests, it played the important role of persuading newcomers or supporters of other doctrines of the rightness of the National Socialist message, this was not its primary function. The chief aim of such gatherings was to absorb the individual into a mass of like-minded people, and the purpose of the 'suggestion' was not to deceive but to articulate that which the crowd already believed. The crowd is of one opinion – Hitler speaks of 'the agreement of thousands'. Its experience is of 'intoxication and enthusiasm', of near-hysterical support for the message.

The function of propaganda was thus not to dupe, but to mobilize what was already latent. More generally, Hitler saw in the National Socialist movement not merely a means to capturing the state with a few misled supporters, but as a voluntarist mobilization of healthy national sentiment:

By 'us' I mean all the hundreds of thousands who fundamentally long for the same thing without as individuals
finding the words to describe outwardly what they inwardly

visualize; for the noteworthy fact about all reforms is
that at first they possess but a single champion yet many
million supporters. Their aim has often been for centuries
the inner longing of hundreds of thousands, until one
man stands up to proclaim such a general will, and as a
standard-bearer guides the old longing to victory in the
form of the new idea.

(MK, 300)

The 'standard-bearer' of the people, the 'one man' who stands
up to proclaim the 'general will' was, we may safely assume,
Hitler himself.

What kind of a state did Hitler envisage as best able to
implement 'the general will'? Hitler is frustratingly vague on
the precise forms that the state would take under National
Socialism. What matters ultimately, he argues, is not whether
the new state has the outward trappings of a monarchy or a
republic but whether it safeguards the essential needs of the
race. The militarist and authoritarian character of the coming
National Socialist state is implicit in Hitler's rejection of pacifism and democracy, as we have seen. We have already
detected totalitarian ambitions in Hitler's insistence that the
needs of the individual were to be subordinated totally to the
vital needs of the race, and in his demands that the state
should intervene ruthlessly to enforce the interests of the
community over its individual members. Other passing references make it clear that the state will be dominant, as when
Hitler argues that 'the NSDAP should not become a consta-
ble of public opinion, but must dominate it. It must not
become a servant of the masses, but their master!' (MK, 422) or
when he informs the reader that National Socialism must
learn 'to force the laws of life [. . .] on the German people despite

all resistance' (2B, 40). The threat of terror is clear in such passages, even if it is not spelled out.

And yet, as Hitler's reflections on propaganda make very clear, he did not see the strength of the state as residing in terror alone. Its strength lay in a combination of its ability to mobilize and to suppress. It served to mobilize those whom he wished to integrate – the healthy members of the 'national community' – and to suppress those who stood outside the community – the enemies of the nation. The terroristic message of *Mein Kampf* is directed overwhelmingly at the enemies of the race – the Marxists and the Jews. But for those willing to open their eyes, including the mass of the workers once they have been liberated from the clutches of the left, the promise is one of social integration and national renewal, pursued through programmes of racial regeneration embraced by the members of the new 'national community'.

It would be wrong, therefore, to see in *Mein Kampf* a simple vision of a terroristic state apparatus of the type commonly associated with the cruder forms of 'totalitarianism' theory. There is in Hitler's writings a more complex vision of the new state – however structured – positioned at the head of a much broader process of national mobilization, and acting as the agent of a biological revival of the race. Terror is one of its tools, but not the only one. More fundamentally, its strength is drawn from the fact that it reflects the demands of healthy popular sentiment.

The sentiments that *Mein Kampf* articulated were, in fact, not so much sentiments as resentments. The book articulated extreme nationalist resentments – against the Treaty of Versailles and against the 'war guilt' clause that the nation had been forced to swallow. It articulated extreme racist resentments – against Poles, but above all against Jews, whom Hitler regarded as a hostile race in fundamental conflict with Germany and out to destroy his people. It articulated extreme political resentments – against Socialists and against Marxists, the so-called 'November criminals' who were to blame for Germany's collapse in 1918 and for the creation of the hated Weimar Republic. And it articulated a more diffuse set of social resentments, such as resentments against the so-called 'ballast existences' of the mentally or physically ill or other socially marginalized groups.

These resentments provided the means through which millions of ordinary Germans explained to themselves the losing of the war, the impact of defeat and the failings of democratic politics in the 1920s. In spreading his messages through propaganda, Hitler was thus telling Germans what they already inwardly knew. The rancour expressed in *Mein Kampf* was nothing but an extreme expression of the more general bitterness felt by millions of Germans experiencing profound disorientation under the burden of the many-headed crisis unleashed upon German society by the First World War. Reeling under the consequences of the collapse of 1918, millions of ordinary Germans chose to focus their resentments on the victorious powers who had defeated them rather than on the bankrupt imperial regime that had led them into the war. Unwilling to recognize that Germany's armies had been defeated in the field, they also chose to blame the Socialists and Marxists who had participated in the revolutionary upheavals at the end of the war. Suffering under the chaotic conditions created by the challenges of demobilization and the destabilizing effect of inflation, they chose to blame the fledgling Republican system that was struggling to cope with these problems. Behind all these sources of discontent they saw, or at least sensed, the Jews.

Anti-Socialism, anti-Marxism, anti-Republicanism and anti-Semitism provided millions of ordinary Germans with the means to make sense of an overwhelming political, economic and cultural crisis. *Mein Kampf*, we may conclude, is a crucial document of that crisis.

# CHRONOLOGY

**20 April 1889**  Birth of Adolf Hitler in Braunau on the Inn

**1907–1913**  Hitler lives in Vienna

**24 May 1913**  Hitler moves to Munich

**August 1914**  Outbreak of First World War

**1914–1918**  Hitler serves in German army; receives Iron Crosses, Second and First Class

**23 October 1918**  Hitler temporarily blinded in gas attack and hospitalized

**November 1918**  Wave of revolutionary activity spreads from northern ports across Germany; Proclamation of Republic; Armistice signed

**5 January 1919**  Foundation of German Workers' Party (DAP); renamed National Socialist German Workers' Party (NSDAP) in 1920

**28 June 1919**  Signing of Treaty of Versailles

**August 1919**  Constitution of the Weimar Republic

**September 1919**  Hitler joins DAP

**July 1921**  Leadership crisis within NSDAP, culminating in Hitler's elevation to position of Party Chairman

**January 1923**  French occupation of the Ruhr

**November 1923**  Hitler leads failed 'Beer-hall Putsch' in Munich

**February–April 1924**  Hitler tried for treason; sentenced to prison for five years

**1924**  First volume of *Mein Kampf* written during imprisonment

**20 December 1924**  Hitler released from prison after serving less than nine months of his term

**February 1925**  Refoundation of NSDAP

**1925–1929**  NSDAP remains fringe party but extends and consolidates position across Germany

**July 1926** Publication of first volume of *Mein Kampf*

**December 1925** Publication of second volume of *Mein Kampf*

**Summer 1928** Writing of *Second Book*, which remains unpublished

**1929–1933** The Depression provides context for radical expansion of NSDAP membership and support

**March 1930** Final Weimar coalition collapses

**March 1930–January 1933** Germany ruled by authoritarian governments of Brüning, Papen, Schleicher

**January 1933** Series of meetings and negotiations between NSDAP leadership, elites and Hindenburg's entourage

**30 January 1933** Hitler appointed Reich Chancellor

**March 1933** Creation of first official concentration camp (Dachau)

**August 1934** Hindenburg dies; Hitler combines offices of President and Chancellor to become 'Führer and Reich Chancellor'

**March 1935** Introduction of Conscription

**15 September 1935** Promulgation of Nuremberg Laws

**7 March 1936** Remilitarization of Rhineland

**November 1936** Proclamation of Rome–Berlin Axis; signature of Anti-Comintern Pact

**5 November 1937** 'Hossbach meeting', at which Hitler's expansionist goals are outlined, and Britain is described as a 'hate-inspired antagonist'

**March 1938** Annexation of Austria

**September 1938** Sudeten Crisis culminates in Munich Conference and acquisition of Sudetenland

**November 1938** 'Night of Glass' (*Kristallnacht*) marks intensification of anti-Jewish campaigns

**30 January 1939** Hitler issues infamous prophecy concerning the fate of the Jews in a new war

**14 March 1939** Germany invades Czechoslovakia, establishing Reich Protectorate of Bohemia and Moravia

**September 1939** Germany invades Poland; Britain and France declare war

**September 1939** *onwards* Jews of Occupied Europe subjected to forced labour, deportation, ghettoization and mass executions

**April 1940** Germany invades Denmark and Norway

**May–June 1940** German campaign against France

**Summer 1940** Battle of Britain

**22 June 1941** Germany invades Soviet Union (Operation Barbarossa); SS-*Einsatzgruppen* initiate murder of Soviet Jews

**20 January 1942** Wannsee Conference finalizes jurisdictional and organizational issues concerning 'Final Solution'

**Spring 1942** The extermination camps commence mass murder

**February 1943** Capitulation of German Sixth Army at Stalingrad

**19 March 1944** German occupation of Hungary, followed by deportation of Hungarian Jews to Auschwitz

**June 1944** Collapse of German positions on Eastern Front; launch of Second Front

**20 July 1944** Assassination attempt on Hitler's life by Claus Schenk von Stauffenberg

**January 1945** Soviet offensive resumed

**27 January 1945** Liberation of Auschwitz

**30 April 1945** Hitler commits suicide in Berlin

**2 May 1945** Berlin captured by Red Army

**8 May 1945** General Keitel surrenders to Marshal Zhukov in Berlin

# SUGGESTIONS FOR FURTHER READING

Of the many biographical studies of Hitler see the following: Alan Bullock, *Hitler: A Study in Tyranny* (London, 1952); Joachim C. Fest, *Hitler* (London, 1973); and, most recently, the magisterial two-volume political biography by Ian Kershaw: *Hitler, 1889–1936: Hubris* (London, 1998) and *Hitler, 1936–1945: Nemesis* (London, 2000).

For interesting reflections on the formation of Hitler's views see also Brigitte Hamann, *Hitler's Vienna: A Dictator's Apprenticeship* (Oxford, 1999). For an earlier attempt to make sense of Hitler's writings in the 1920s that still holds much interest see Eberhard Jäckel, *Hitler's World-View: A Blueprint for Power* (Middletown, Conn., 1972). Roger Griffin, *The Nature of Fascism* (London, 1991) is a challenging but stimulating attempt to locate the common elements of fascist ideology and has an excellent section on Hitler and Nazism.

Two recent studies of Germany in the First World War which highlight just how far from the truth Hitler's depictions of the home-front experience were are: Jeffrey Verhey, *The Spirit of 1914: Militarism, Myth and Mobilization in Germany* (Cambridge, 2000) and Belinda J. Davis, *Home Fires Burning: Food, Politics and Everyday Life in World War I Berlin* (North Carolina, 2000).

There is, unfortunately, no recent study in English of the 1918–19 German revolution, but a good introduction to the subject is provided in the opening sections of Hans Mommsen, *The Rise and Fall of Weimar Democracy* (Chapel, Hill, 1996). For those wishing to read further on Hitler's rise to power against the wider backdrop of Germany in the 1920s, by far the best recent survey is Richard J. Evans, *The Coming of the Third Reich* (London, 2003).

For introductions to the experience of Germany's Jews in the modern era see Volumes 3 and 4 of Michael Meyer and Michael Brenner (eds.), *German-Jewish History in Modern Times* – Vol. 3, *Integration in Dispute 1871–1918* (New York, 1997) and Vol. 4, *Renewal and Destruction, 1918–1945* (New York, 1998).

For introductions to the changing ways in which historians have interpreted the phenomenon of Hitler and Nazism see Ian Kershaw, *The Nazi Dictatorship: Problems and Perspectives of Interpretation* (London, 4th edn., 2000) and Neil Gregor (ed.), *Nazism: A Reader* (Oxford, 2000).

Websites on Hitler, Nazi Germany and the Holocaust which are poor, or misleading greatly outnumber those which are reliable and helpful. Those which appear to be the most serious are often the most mendacious. Readers wishing to make use of internet resources are strongly advised to stick with sites which have been recommended by established, respected institutions or organizations. The following may be recommended (each contains extensive further links):

United States Holocaust Memorial Museum: http://www.ushmm.org
Yad Vashem: http://www.yad-vashem.org.il/
Beth Shalom, UK: http://www.bethshalom.com
Holocaust Education Trust: http://www.het.org.uk/index.htm

# INDEX